EDUCATION INTO RELIGION

EDUCATION INTO RELIGION

By

A. VICTOR MURRAY

PRESIDENT OF CHESHUNT COLLEGE, CAMBRIDGE
EMERITUS PROFESSOR OF EDUCATION,
UNIVERSITY COLLEGE, HULL

NEW YORK
HARPER AND BROTHERS · PUBLISHERS

PREFACE

I f it were not that the word "rationale" is felt nowadays to be both pompous and cumbersome, I should have called this book "The Rationale of the Teaching of the Christian Religion", for that is what it is. Before anyone can be turned loose to teach anything to anybody, he (or she) ought to know why he is doing it, what he hopes to achieve by it, how he ought to do it, what are the difficulties in the road, and, as the Americans say (unconsciously translating the word "rationale" into colloquial English), what is the "big idea" behind the whole thing. These questions this book attempts to answer.

The present title of the book contains its thesis. It is a discussion of the nature of education when its goal is religion. Christianity is here viewed not as a *corpus* of historical documents and dogmatic statements which the pupil has to learn in order to become religious. It is an attitude to life *into* which he has to grow.

Religious education, therefore, when the religion is Christianity, is the most difficult type of education because its ultimate goal is a certain quality of life and a personal loyalty to Christ. There is no short cut to this achievement, although many have been tried. In the second chapter we shall look at a number of these attempts. In this as in other fields, however, it is quite impossible to rely on any mechanical device to do for us that which can be done only by persons. Moreover, in religious education itself, if it is to be distinguished from proselytism and propaganda, there are involved certain theological and also psychological considerations which must be adequately appreciated if there is to be any approximation to success. And these in turn require an appreciation of the limitations of religious education as well as of its possibilities.

Where the line is to be drawn is by no means easy to

determine, and it is not made easier by the bland assurance with which fundamentalists and totalitarians on the one hand and modernists on the other approach their task. It is my belief that it is quite impossible to state the problem, let alone to solve it, unless the theological issues are squarely faced. It is to this task that the book is addressed. And in so far as it is of little value to discuss these matters purely as theological questions, I have all the time had in mind specific situations and practical problems. As these have arisen chiefly in my own experience they are necessarily illustrated from English conditions, but the chapters in the book were delivered in the first instance as lectures in Canada and the illustrations were found to be not irrelevant to the American and Canadian situation. The fact that in England the great bulk of religious education is done in the day schools of the nation while across the Atlantic it is done by the Churches alone does not really affect the historical, doctrinal and psychological issues that are involved. These are present in any case.

With regard to these local references, however, there is perhaps one unexpected justification for taking them from the English scene, especially in Chapter III. It is no more than the truth to say that England is in a fair way to a solution of a problem which has long vexed both educationists and Church authorities in America. The problem concerns the place of religious education in the public or national schools.

The founding fathers of the American republic were no doubt wise in their generation when they followed the Virginia Statute of 1786 and made a formal separation of Church and State. One of the consequences, however, is characterized by Dean Sperry of Harvard as "the rank growth of denominationalism."[1] There is difficulty in conceiving of Christianity itself except in a denominational form. Religious education, being entirely in the hands of the Churches, almost necessarily takes that form also, and clearly it would be impossible to have religious education in

[1] *Religion in America*, by Willard L. Sperry. Cambridge Press, 1945, p. 43.

the schools if it involved dividing off children according to their
denominations and having the teaching done by every sect that
was represented. This is a consideration which has not been
absent from discussion of the same problem even in England.

The difficulty, however, in so far as it relates to Bible
teaching, belongs to the period before the days of the historical
method. I think it is sober truth that the historical method
has made possible an educational use of the Bible into which
no denominational considerations whatever need enter.
There is, nevertheless, a considerable time lag between the
acceptance of this method in the divinity faculties of the
universities and its acceptance or even the realization of its
existence by the ordinary church member or the ordinary
teacher of religion, or even, in America, the ordinary
Director of Religious Education. In England the same time lag
still exists but it is rapidly shrinking. It has shrunk enough
by now to enable a situation to arise in which the children
of the nation can have their religious education in the schools
of the nation and based on syllabuses drawn up by agreement
between the teachers, the churches, and the statutory local
authorities. It was symbolic of this state of affairs that when
the latest Cambridgeshire Syllabus (1949) was published it
was solemnly dedicated by the Bishop of Ely at a service in
Great St. Mary's Church in Cambridge, in which Anglican
and Free Church ministers and teachers took part, and a
copy of the book was formally presented by the chairman of
the local County Council to the bishop who laid it on the
altar. There was nothing denominational in this act of
worship any more than there was anything denominational
about the book itself, but it was a definitely Christian service
all the same.

It is worth while therefore to draw illustrations from this
English situation because it is a witness to the fact that
except for Roman Catholics the denominational issue has
no real relevance in the matter of religious instruction in
schools. We can get on quite well without it. What is
required, however, is an acceptance of the historical method

of study. There is no doubt a good deal of so-called "undenominational" religious teaching both in England and in America which is so because it avoids the cardinal theological issue and concerns itself only with technique, and not always very good technique. But the English experience has shown not only that there is no need to evade the theological issue in this way, but also that deliberate evasion does despite to the very subject that we are trying to teach. It is the confusion of the theological issue with the denominational issue which leads to such evasion.

But the facing of the real issue will be a hard task, and perhaps much harder in America than in Britain, because it means accepting both for the Faith itself and for education the challenge that is inherent in Fundamentalism. It should be made quite clear that Fundamentalism is not an alternative method of studying Scripture as it did not matter which you choose. It is on the contrary a mis-handling of Scripture and has been the root cause of so many sects and divisions among us. When men substitute for the sober, objective, historical study of the word of God a method which allows as fair comment on Scripture anything that chimes in with their own prejudice (and this applies to all schools of thought and not only to Fundamentalists) the way is open for sectarian controversy and every kind of proselytism and propaganda.

I trust therefore that what has been said here is not irrelevant to either denominational or Sunday schools even where the illustrations are drawn from English Council Schools. Nor, I hope, have I lost sight of the fact that there are still very many homes in which religious education is given by the parents—perhaps the best way of all, if the parents are really free to give it. I have attempted to be a kind of middleman between the experts in scholarship whether theological or Biblical and the ordinary teacher in school, the director of religious education in a church and the parent in the home. Some of the earlier Agreed Syllabuses in England suffered from the fact that they were drawn up mainly by university experts who, through no fault of their own, had no contact with the schools. Teachers attending summer courses were often greatly inspired by the scholars but were even more helpless when it came to interpreting all this material to 10- or 14-year-olds in a Council School. It will clearly be some years before we have enough teachers of this subject whose standard of knowledge and method is at least equal to that of teachers in the more usual subjects.

The chapters in this book first took shape as lectures given at Emmanuel College, Toronto, at the request of the United Church of Canada Training School for Women. They were given under the general title of "The theological foundations of religious education". To the Principal of that school, Mrs. Jean Hutchinson, and the theological staff at Emmanuel I am most grateful for the opportunity given and for their unfailing kindness. In their final form the lectures have been given as open lectures in the University of Cambridge by the courtesy of the Faculty of Divinity. Two chapters contain large sections from an earlier work, *The School and the Church*, which has been long out of print, and I am grateful to the publishers (the Student Christian Movement) for kindly allowing me to incorporate them here.

I have been honoured and gratified by having had the manuscript read and criticized by my friend Professor Clement C. J. Webb. At an advanced age his mind is no less keen and illuminating than it was forty years ago when I was an undergraduate and he was a tutor at Magdalen College, Oxford. He would not agree with all that is set down here and he is in no way responsible for it but I have certainly profited by his criticism as well as by the stimulus of his long friendship.

As on many a previous occasion my wife has very kindly checked the proof copy and made it more presentable and perhaps also more intelligible.

A. V. M.

Cambridge.
March 31, 1953

The Biblical references are mainly to the English Revised Version, which is readily accessible, if now less accurate, than the Revised Standard Versions published in 1946 and 1952.

by ELTON TRUEBLOOD

The publication of Victor Murray's great book is an important event. Not for a long time has the thoughtful reader had the chance to consider the problems of religious education with the help of a disciplined mind that is, at the same time, reverent, philosophical and practical. We have countless books on educational theory, we have a good many on the work of the church school, and our time has been marked by a tough-minded theology, but it is the combination of these interests that is rare. Professor Murray, who has read widely and thought much, has obviously poured into this volume the fruits of a lifetime of work and the result is a treatment remarkable both for its maturity and its wholeness.

The reader who comes to this book expecting to find a detailed treatment of how religion may be taught in the secular school, in the home or in the church school will be surprised and perhaps even disappointed. The book may be deeply helpful in all three of these important enterprises, but the teacher or parent will not be given a blueprint. What he will be given, instead, is a wise and thorough consideration of the ways in which lives are changed, or current fallacies to be avoided, of the nature of standards, of the growth of character. And if he reads carefully to the end, he will be glad that he has been given what Professor Murray has given us, instead of something easier and cheaper. The subject of the book may be termed, accurately, The Philosophy of Moral and Religious Education.

The average reader will have reason to be glad that the author has disciplined himself sufficiently to write in such a way that the ordinary literate person can understand what he says. In a day when so many shallow waters are muddied to make them look deep, it is a pleasure to find a writer who has been willing to do the extra intellectual work to achieve clarity. The book, fortunately, is free from all jargon of the academic sects and likewise free from any particular jargon of its own.

One result of this clarity, which so marks the author's style, is the high quotability of many of the sentences. If the book secures the American reading which it deserves it is likely that many of these sentences will be quoted often and with profit. Consider the pithiness of the following: "Vices do not become virtues because they are indulged in the name of religion." Or this: "To claim infallibility in the affairs of God, who is from everlasting to everlasting, is to fall into the sin of that familiarity which is contempt."

The illustrations, in which the discussion abounds, are largely British, but this does not mean that the book is inapplicable to the North American situation. The relations between the religious forces and the secular schools are not the same in any of the countries in the Atlantic community, but the main principles enunciated in this book are applicable to all, whether the readers are in England, Scotland, Canada or the United States. All of us are faced with the dangers of a militantly secularized society as well as the special problems which denominationalism raises. Many will be grateful, in this connection, to Professor Murray when they find that he refuses to join in the popular clamor against denominations. The ideal, he holds, is the situation in which we are *loyal* to one, while *courteous* to the others.

The author has no good word to say for neutralism, either in morality or religion. The person who loftily claims to be above the battle, superior to all denominations or political parties, will be denied the understanding of *any*. This is because truth is discoverable only when there is decision. The author argues convincingly that no moral issue has been faced at all unless and until we make up our minds and proceed to action. Thus we may be sure that the study of comparative religions, fashionable in the recent past, is a very poor substitute for the understanding of *one* to which the individual is devoted and which he tries, in spite of recurrent failure, to practice. In the deepest matters there is something far better than cool detachment; at some point a man, of whatever age, must make the leap of faith. Those who never make it never understand even what they are missing.

All this leads to what is most original in the book: the careful consideration of the education of the emotions. Far from fearing the emotional life, Professor Murray recognizes that it is necessary, not only for ordinary living, but for intellectual achievement as well. Our emotional powers, like our consciences, are highly educable, and any education which omits this aspect is guilty of gross neglect. The author knows that the emotions must be guided and disciplined rather than repressed and he says some highly valuable things about the development of self-discipline in the child. At this point he becomes openly practical and suggests concrete steps which the wise parent or teacher may wish to follow.

Many readers will be pleased with the way in which our author avoids easy answers. He never suggests that there is a Christian pattern of conduct which we follow specifically once we see the pattern. The character of Jesus is, indeed, the standard of Christian morality, but it is never a simple matter to know what Jesus would do here and now. Discouraging as it may seem, we have to work out the details for ourselves. This we must do, not in the light of some isolated text, but in the light of Christ's whole life and ministry as these have been made available to us. Above all, we must follow Christ's own example in dealing with questions *as they arise* and in the light of the particular situation in the individual case. Thus the author rejects casuistry, by which he means the attempt to solve moral problems before they have arisen.

There are two ways by which men and women achieve the sensitiveness of spirit which enable them to understand something of the will of God. One way is that of a cataclysmic conversion and the other is education. Because, for millions of our day, it will, apparently, have to be the latter or nothing, the educational enterprise is of great importance in our religious life. The task of the educator is far more difficult than is that of the engineer or the mechanic, and he cannot be as definite in his conclusions, but because his task is truly great he must never cease in his quest.

This quest is the interest of many in the modern world and all who follow it can be helped by this book if they will use it in the right way. They must read it slowly, they must stop and think, they must underline, and then think again. If parents, teachers and pastors come to the book in this way, its publication is good news.

CONTENTS

Page

CHAPTER VII. STANDARDS 117

CHAPTER VIII. DOCTRINE 141

CHAPTER IX. SCEPTICISM AND INFALLIBILITY . . 163

CHAPTER X. THE CHRISTIAN COMMUNITY . . 178

CHAPTER XI. THE EDUCATION OF THE EMOTIONS: (2) WORSHIP

201

CHAPTER XII. FUNDAMENTAL AIMS 214

CHAPTER I

THE DILEMMA OF RELIGIOUS EDUCATION

I

THE phrase "religious education" is almost self-contradictory, for it seems to join together two opposites which all experience has put asunder. It is held that education proceeds by enquiry, criticism and experiment; religion is a matter of faith, obedience and tradition. Education concerns the intellect; the root of religion is feeling. Education has to do with the world here and now; religion has its vital interest in the unseen world of spirit. Education requires teaching; religion is "caught not taught". Education is concerned with the slow amelioration of our earthly lot, whereas religion in one aspect represents the challenge to alter it here and now. Education is identified with the humanist outlook and the best "pagan" virtues; religion advocates sacrifice and discipline.

These distinctions are apt to be misleading, for there is a sense in which whatever is postulated of education is equally true of a historical religion and vice versa. A very considerable part of the task of education is to transmit tradition. But it is well to remember that the fact that the distinctions are made at all is due not necessarily to self-will and frowardness but to the inescapable truth that we have to struggle with eternal verities within the bounds of our mortality. Can ultimate reality be apprehended within the limitations of flesh and blood, of time and sense? From what point are we to begin our search after God? Shall we more certainly succeed if we begin with ourselves as the only facts of which we have first-hand knowledge, and from ourselves work up to God, or shall we begin with God, or rather our idea of Him, as the highest standard which we can conceive, and so work downwards to a more critical judgment of ourselves? Each of these ways has been trodden by great saints and great scholars from the beginning of Christian history, and there seems no likelihood that either road will ever be closed. They represent not merely approaches to truth but also the convictions by which men have lived and saved their souls alive, and both are religious.

All this is natural, inevitable and healthy, and this kind of controversy cannot and ought not to be avoided. Neither ought it to be overlaid by or identified with modern party disputes. We have passed altogether away from the region of wholesome argument once we insist that our own point of view is the only reasonable one, or that it is at any rate a kind of blazing light to which other people's convictions are simply farthing candles. When men in defence of their party interests stiffen their sinews, summon up their blood and imitate the action of the tiger, they are scarcely in a mood to recognize the truth even when they see it.

Nevertheless these distinctions create a dilemma for "religious education". How can such a hybrid exist? How can it be at one and the same time both "religious" and "education"?

Religion in the Christian sense has to do with those experiences in which the soul of man knows itself to stand for the time being in the presence of God. It is at bottom a personal relationship even though it may be experienced in a crowded place of worship. It is the concern of two parties in what Brünner calls "the divine-human encounter". The intrusion of a third party takes from it its most characteristic feature. "We die alone", said Pascal, but he might well have added that in the most intimate regions of our being we also live alone. The vision of God is for all men, and Christ may appear as he did in Galilee to "over five hundred brethren at once",[1] but each man knows it to be his own vision and that the eternal controversy that God has with man requires an individual answer.

[1] I Corinthians xv. 6.

This being so, where does education come in? For education ordinarily implies precisely this intruding third party—the teacher. He is the middleman who takes upon himself the priestly function of mediating the things of God to those who, he thinks, imperfectly apprehend them. Certainly there are things to learn in religion, especially where that religion is so vitally concerned with the events of history as is Christianity. We have to know its origins, the nature of its message, its institutions and the course of its history. But we may know all this without having religion itself. Knowledge of religious history and doctrine does not of itself bring a man into the presence of God—it may even make him content to stay where he is. Something is required in the man himself which no teacher can ever supply. There comes a point where some sort of personal commitment is necessary and without which no further growth in knowledge is possible. Education, like the Law, may be the *paidagogos* to bring a man to Christ, but it can only bring him there.

It is true, therefore, that there is a final distinction between education and religion (although the point of difference is much farther off than we sometimes think it is), and the phrase "religious education" may easily conceal a confusion. Men may use it without at all realizing the dilemma contained within it. And yet we cannot escape either the idea or the thing itself.

As far back as we can go in human development there has always been religious education. No primitive tribe has yet been discovered which did not have its religious initiation, its *rites de passage*. Religion is never simply an uninformed emotion. Wherever found it possesses content, tradition, externality, sacrament, something that is personally communicable. It is only among highly sophisticated people that it can be thought of as lacking these things and as something purely subjective. Its concern is always with the unseen God; and how do we know who God is, and what is His nature? For answers to these questions we have in a measure to depend on other people and on the accumulated experience

B

of the past, and our knowledge of all this involves education. The problem is, how can we set our minds to work concerning God without at the same time allowing religious education itself to become a substitute for religion? Knowledge can so easily stand proxy for faith, and sophistication can prevent the growth of character.

This is what might be called the philosophical dilemma and whatever happens this still remains. But there is also the pressing practical question, for if we accept the fact that there must be religious education, we have then to discover how best to give it. Who, for instance, are the people best qualified for this task? It is easy to say that *of course* the professionally religious man, the parson, is the obvious person. But is education really the parson's job? Is he not, above all others, the man whose appeal is to faith and authority, and is not his concern with worship and church membership rather than with education? Besides, even if we, and he, grant that for a historical religion education is necessary, is he an adept at educational method? Have we not all endured those "children's addresses" given to children of all ages lumped together—a procedure you would never adopt with mathematics or history?

Is then the professional teacher the best person to give it? He knows, or ought to know, about child psychology and grading, and he may also "know his Bible". But is that all that there is to it? May he not require not more knowledge but an altogether different angle of approach?

And then there are special aspects of the problem which arise from the varying traditions of different countries. In England, for instance, by the Act of 1944 all children in the nation's schools are given religious instruction as a regular part of the school curriculum and the syllabus is drawn up under the direction of the administrative authority. Religion is the concern of the State in Spain also but for a totally different reason and with a totally different end in view. In the United States and Canada, on the other hand, separation of Church and State is so firmly written into the Constitution that religious education cannot be given by the State at all but is a matter for the churches alone.

The basic fact remains, however, that a historical religion requires teaching by somebody, whether by teachers or by parsons, whether by the Church alone or in the schools of the nation. An illiterate inhabitant of a desert island might, like the "poor Indian",

> see God in clouds or hear him in the wind,

and he might be and probably would be a very religious man, but he could never become a Christian in that way. To be a Christian involves knowing about Christ and about the Bible and with no one to teach him he could never know anything about either. Teaching, therefore, is necessary, and yet the goal is something beyond teaching. We are concerned with the spirit of man himself responding to the presence of God, and how can that be "taught"?

2

We shall be concerned here chiefly with Christianity, and in Christianity there are two main streams of "revelation" which are the subject matter for religious education.

First of all there is that which it shares with the Jews and which produced the Old Testament Scriptures. Here, beginning from a common marshy pool of animism, a clear stream of spiritual religion slowly made a channel for itself as it went along. Many of its ideas were completely unexpected and even unwanted by the very men who gave them to the world. The ideas were not invented by them: they were wrung out of them. A God that is infinitely kinder and more just than man, a God who is nevertheless exacting in His standards of purity and truth, a God who enters into men's lives and suffers with them, a God who longs for the love of men but never forces it—these were Old Testament discoveries. They informed the sense of God and gave to it a name and a character. The marsh became a well-defined river.

And whenever these discoveries have been re-discovered, as they have been all down the ages as well as over again in the life-history of the individual, they sound the depths of human nature as if all along we had been waiting for just this.

Indeed this is the other side of the experience that we call conversion—recognition that we have suddenly discovered something that was all the while there had we but known it. Hence the revelation of God is not a generalization in which we sum up the course of history, nor is it a mechanical deposit of propositions in which certain people believe; it is a living experience of living people which speaks to our condition and is continually being re-enacted in the lives of men. Indeed it is precisely this power of fresh re-creation which marks it out as a "revelation" at all.

It is obvious, therefore, that "knowledge of God" is something that is capable of education and that we are able to learn more and more of Him with whom we have to do.

The second revelation familiar to us in Christianity is that of Jesus Christ.

Here again we find something quite unexpected. How a young carpenter of Nazareth could have been so completely at home in the region of timeless truth and have had so strong a hold on the love and power of God as to have been identified in nature with Him, and how He should have been misunderstood by His own people, hounded to death by them, and then, lo! a real miracle, and He continues in the world alive for evermore, affecting alien centuries, alien tongues and alien customs, turning men in all ages from darkness to light, and "from the power of Satan unto God"—none of this can be explained by any "natural" causes whatever. No doubt both orthodoxy and liberalism have done their best to explain it, the one by making it turn on a special kind of physical birth, and the other by making Jesus the focus of contemporary forces already at work, but these attempts are quite inadequate to explain and still more to explain away the single most important fact in the history of man upon this earth.

Now the story of Jesus is a matter of history, and we cannot know about Him unless some other person or some book tells us. There is no other way of finding out. We have, in other words, to be taught.

There is thus in the development of religion a necessary intermediate place for education. We begin with vague yet powerful premonitions of a spiritual world. "The starry sky above and the moral law within" alike make us aware of it. They are intimations of an immortality, if not for ourselves at any rate for the spiritual realm in which we find ourselves. This, if you care to call it so, is the "religious instinct" in man.

Then through the history of the race and in the experience of the individual it comes to be "informed". This "informing", however, is not just a matter of anybody's idle speculation concerning the nature of the universe and the problems of life and destiny. Irresponsible speculation has always been a fruitful source of superstition, and where it has acquired social sanctions it has led to malice, hatred and uncharitableness. The informing, however, of religious feeling comes about only by that kind of reflection which has kept closely in touch with the feeling itself, when men in fear and trembling have worked out their own salvation, but knowing all the while that it is God that worketh in them "both to will and to do of His good pleasure". In a historical religion, particularly in Judaism and in Christianity, religious feeling has been associated by reflective men with events that took place in time. Accordingly, to understand a religion of this kind and to share in it require education.

There is, however, a further stage. Religious feeling thus informed becomes aware of itself, and the religious man realizes that it is only in a God whose nature we best understand through Jesus Christ—who is, so to speak, the "Father" of Jesus Christ—and that it is in His will, hidden from us though it is, that we find our peace. Thus knowledge derived from history is verified in experience, and so makes keener that sense of God with which we begin. Religion, even in its most intellectual form, where it is sincere, is always in the last

resort intuitive. But, as in all other psychological development, so also in this, that which is learned comes to feel just as
instinctive as that which requires no learning. Indeed it
becomes even more instinctive, and the life of the truly
educated Christian is governed so effectively by those
considerations which appear to the outsider to be purely
historical that they take precedence even unconsciously over
those forces which are prior in development but no longer
prior in importance. In other words, history becomes
transmuted into character.

3

Education is clearly necessary to religion. But is religion
equally necessary to education? It has been the fashion of
recent years to believe that it is not, and indeed to think that
education may be a substitute for religion. For it is said that
education trains men to think, to criticize, to experiment,
and to control the world in which they find themselves,
whereas religion appears to offer chiefly a thrill. This thrill
may come in the excitement of mass emotion, or in solitary
self-abasement before the altar, but it is the business of the
educated man to get away from the tyranny of thrills and
preserve himself whole and intelligent. Thrills are altogether
inimical to the development of the prudential virtues, just
as they get in the way of any intelligent view of the universe.
Thus runs the argument. But here again we are dealing with
but a partial experience. It altogether ignores the fact that a
religion that is historical, that is to say, one that is concerned
with actual events, must be very much more than a thrill.

A further contrast is often made to show how unnecessary
religion is to education. If it is true that "we needs must love
the highest when we see it" (and many people believed that,
at any rate before the war), then all we require is that we shall
be enabled to see it. Religion, therefore, is not necessary
in the field of morals. This identification of virtue with
knowledge is as old as Plato and as recent as H. G. Wells.

If it were true, then the way to build up a man's character would be to give him more education.

But is it really true that to know is to do? Is not one of the sad weaknesses of human nature just this inability to love the highest even when we do see it? "The good that I would I do not: but the evil which I would not that I do" was the confession of a greater expert on the human heart than either Plato or H. G. Wells. This helplessness of men in the hour of their keenest insight is unfortunately only too common. Some underpinning is needed to the structure of human life to make it withstand the attacks of the enemy even after we have recognized him for what he is.

Where are we to look for this foundation? There is surely a parable for all life in the fact that the disciples of Christ, who above all other men had the opportunity of loving the highest when they saw it, nevertheless acted against their better judgement and their most passionately avowed conviction when they all forsook Him and fled. And it was not until He was gone and their hold on Him had to be by faith and not by sight that the power came into them to withstand far greater shocks and much more subtle occasions of disloyalty. It is not our hold upon education that will enable us to stand in the evil day and "having done all to stand", but our hold on religion.

There is a historical side to this last consideration. The characteristic belief of the last half of the eighteenth century, put into an educational shape by Rousseau, was the infinite perfectibility of man through education. This is a position which many people, Christians as well as non-Christians, have held, even when they have not expressed it in this way. It is very attractive and flattering to human nature. But there are times when even the most optimistic among us very much doubt it, for we are aware that the ape and the tiger have not yet died within us. It is of course radically opposed to the Christian doctrine of sin, and this may constitute for some people its real charm. To think of sin as something which men grow out of is a quite different doctrine from that which considers sin as a terrible force from which men need to be delivered. Moreover, on the large scale, the moral setback of recent times, the horrors of persecution and the torture chamber have exhibited "sin" as a far more radical and persistent evil than anything that can be removed by educational methods.

All these difficulties in the way of our understanding the relation of education and religion are due at bottom to our ignoring the fact that neither man's life nor his knowledge is bounded by things here and now. The spiritual and eternal impulses within us are for ever struggling with the finite and material bonds which enclose them. No solution which does not take full account of the strength of each factor will ever be satisfactory.

Moreover, even in the external world of time and sense with which we are most familiar we sooner or later come across the existence of an unknown region just as we do within our own hearts. The "within" is also "beyond" and the "beyond" is also "within". After we have striven to search out causes and effects we find sooner or later that everything issues in mystery. The fundamental questions of whence we came and where we go, of origin and of destiny, have still to be asked in every discipline of the mind, whether it be science or history or mathematics or literature or anything else. In any study that we take up we finally come to the threshold of the unknown. Education may postpone our arrival at this threshold, but it brings us there at last, and there it has to leave us.

Neither in the life of man, however, nor in the perfection of human learning has the last word been said when we have exhibited the upward search of our souls for God, whether to satisfy our own spiritual hunger or to obtain a clearer understanding of the world in which we live. If this were all, we might stand on that threshold for ever with the light behind us and the dark before. But while religion needs education and education needs religion, the cardinal differences between them is that religion is concerned with the divine initiative.

God does something on his own part. We come to the threshold and He pulls us through. It is in His light that we see further light.

Is this, however, a fair description of your experience or mine? Probably not. We read about it in the experience of the saints, but it does not appear to happen nowadays. If it does not it is not because past times were different from ours, or because our ancestors were made differently from ourselves. People have been made the same all down the ages. The reason, I think, is that we so rarely get to the threshold of the unknown, either in our thinking or in our human extremity. So long as we think that the sole business of education is to make things clear, so long shall we delay our discovery of the meaning of life.

Things which have to be discovered by education will not be discovered by any other means, but neither can the things that are undiscoverable by education be discovered by it. There is a very profound truth in the popular though rightly criticized attitude to God as someone whom we call in only when all else fails. That is precisely where He does come in— after we have done all that man can do. Unfortunately we are so anxious to believe that man can do everything that we insist on staying to enjoy our own light as long as possible instead of going on to the rim of the dark. The *profound* student, the *profound* philosopher is never irreligious, for he has arrived at the threshold of mystery and can go no farther. It is the half-educated man, the self-satisfied, the successful, the cynic and the smart epigrammatist, those who have not yet arrived at the place where God can take the initiative, who have the glib short answers to the problems of the ages.

It is, however, not only knowledge in the sense of what used to be called "secular" learning that may create the illusion of its own self-sufficiency and keep us away from the boundaries of mystery: this habit of mind is also induced by "religion" itself. The real spiritual danger inherent in the study of theology is that of familiarizing us with that which can never be familiar. When one looks, for example, at the detailed blue-prints of the eternal world exhibited with such assurance in Roman Catholic manuals, or at the minute distinctions within the "plan of salvation" so lovingly dwelt upon by Puritan commentators, one wonders whence they have all come!

Yet the source of all is the same. It is in the persistent unwillingness to let well alone, the refusal to allow God to run the universe on His own lines, the assumption that we are the favoured recipients of His special confidence. The reasoning of such apologists may appear to be historical, but it has nothing to do with history, and the results are as flattering to men's self-esteem as the most ingenious hypotheses of scientists. Yet here again the profound theologian, like the profound student or any other student, is saved from the fatal illusion of finality by the recognition of his own impotence and ignorance. The spiritual world exists in its own right, and it stands to reason that processes which are valid in the world of human thought and action cease to have relevance when we arrive at the threshold. It *has* a law of its own and a certainty of its own, but it is the certainty not of sight but of insight, the law not of knowledge but of faith.

4

There is an advantage in regarding religious education as a dilemma and not merely as a practical problem, because it emphasizes the fact that there is truth as well as error on *both* sides of the argument. To give instruction alone, or to rely on atmosphere alone, will fail. To trust to schools alone or to trust to the clergy alone will fail for the same reason. The real task is to bring all the factors together in such a way as to neutralize the error entirely while conserving the good on both sides. Can it be done?

The question seems to me to be put into its proper setting if we recollect two facts.

The first is that Christianity is a historical religion. As a

religion it is a matter of personal experience of the unseen, and
a personal acceptance of divine sanctions of conduct. This is a
position to which we come through the mere fact that we are
men at all; it is the common matrix out of which all the
religions of the world, including Christianity, have been
fashioned. At the same time, however, as a historical religion
it is vitally concerned with the world of time and sense. It
is a deposit of events, and we therefore need to be informed
about those events. They are external to us.

The second fact to recall is that religious experience,
like other forms of experience, involves continual re-
interpretation. At the beginning it may be no more than a
sense of the presence of God in nature and in oneself, but, as we
have seen, there are stages of religious development, and they
give a clue to the stages of religious education. They are not
necessarily in the same sequence in which they have occurred
in history, for they are levels of interpretation of experience.
Religious education is concerned both with the deepening of
that sense of Heaven which lies about us in our infancy, and
also with the translation into the categories of eternal life of
those great moments of joy and pain, of temptation and
victory, of insight and despair which come to us in our
passage through the world. The historical form with which
we then clothe these experiences, their explanation, for
instance, in the light of the Bible or the lives of the saints, has
in itself very high educational value, although apart from the
experience which it thus informs it may be of no religious
significance to the person concerned.

During these intellectualizing processes a great deal of
religious emotion is either lost or inhibited, and hence
religion and education often appear superficially to be more
in opposition to one another than they really are. This,
however, is not a specifically *religious* difficulty—it is a
consequence of every kind of intellectualizing of an experience.
Our duty is to persevere through this stage, remembering
that the perfection of every intellectual process is feeling.
Sooner or later there is a recovery of religious feeling, but at a

deeper level, for when it is recovered it is no longer a vague, aching sense of the Infinite but a glad joy at being at home in our Father's house with a certain amount of understanding of what is going on.

Thus these levels of religious development are not merely stages of childhood. They may and do occur at any stage of life as the need arises.

5

At this point, therefore, I must make clear the nature and scope of the Christian religion as I understand it, for this will be regulative of our whole treatment.

In the full-orbed Christian faith there seem to me to be five elements. There is something to know, something to feel, something to choose, something to do and something to belong to. Knowledge, feeling, morals, action and belonging are all involved.

(i) Christianity is a historical religion. Therefore we must have recourse to history. The Old and New Testaments are the basic documents of the faith and they are historical records without which there could be no Christian faith at all. Clearly, therefore, instruction in these documents is part of Christian education.

(ii) The root of all religion is feeling, by which I mean not an emotional excitement but rather a deep sense of personal concern with the unseen world. It is something that profoundly matters and so it involves much more than historical knowledge. It brings a man into touch with the world of spirit, and whether at the primitive stage when religion is a worship of mysterious natural agents such as the sky and the thunder, or at the advanced stage in the Eucharist or in meditation upon the Scripture, there is always this sense of *otherness*. Knowledge about God is a matter of study and instruction; knowledge *of* God comes by feeling and intuition, not opposed to the intellectual process (although often assumed to be) but completing it, and informing and disciplining it.

Without this, religion is mere speculation or antiquarianism.

(iii) Christianity also involves moral choice. There is a warfare in human life, and the fact of sin is inescapable. There are conflicts of ideals and of loyalties both within and without the human soul itself. If men are not aware of sin in themselves they cannot but be aware of it in the world of nations and classes. On which side, therefore, are we going to stand? The ancient prophet thundered out to his people, "Choose ye this day whom ye will serve", and this demand with even greater insistence is at the heart of the Christian Gospel. No man can serve two masters. The choice of "either/or" has to be made by the Christian, and to refuse to make a choice or to be blind to the existence of alternatives is more than a misunderstanding. It is a moral defect.

(iv) Then action is needed. Luther may have felt that the Epistle of James was an "epistle of straw" because of its insistence that "faith without works is dead", but it represents a vital part of the Gospel. For a man to be concerned only with his own personal salvation leads to a morbid interest in his own sensations and theories. If love is the characteristic of the Christian religion it must express itself in loving, that is to say, in personal relationships, in an attitude to society, in practical service to and concern for other people. The Gospel gives short shrift to those who ignore the brother for whom Christ died, or refuse to feed the hungry, clothe the naked or visit the prisoner.

Action, however, has another aspect not so commonly recognized but of great value in human experience and in education. The externalizing of an emotion helps to prevent it becoming morbid and also to recall it when it has gone. This is the psychological importance of ritual and drama and worship. They are forms of action not alternative to experience or conviction but closely associated with it. Two men who have quarrelled may come to a reconciliation through speech or correspondence, but shaking hands is almost a necessary ritual. It is more than an outward and visible sign of goodwill—it is itself a means of promoting it. It is in the truest sense of the words a "means of grace", a sacrament.

(v) Christianity has come down to us through the agency of the Christian community. It is that community which has preserved the Scriptures and developed tradition and codified experience. Moreover, the life of that community is in intention a challenge to the world, for here the social values of the kingdom of God are cherished and embodied. The fact that the practice so far lags behind the theory does not disparage the theory; it is a witness to the truth of the New Testament view that the kingdom of God is both here now and is yet to come. In Christ we believe we have the full revelation of God, and each generation finds it to be so, but its fullness is itself in process of being revealed. "God has yet more light and truth to break forth from his word." And the Christian community is an essential part of the Gospel, for it is through the life and witness of the community that Christ is made known to men.

Even the man who is converted by a text owes the preservation of that text to the Christian community and must seek within the Christian community an opportunity for further light and a field of service. There is no other religion in which the believing community is itself a part of its gospel, self-critical of its own shortcomings and looking forward to a continual amplification of its message and significance. "Belonging" is an essential part of the Christian faith.

The significance of these aspects of the faith for religious education is that they represent also different modes of Christian experience.

> There is no expeditious road
> To pack and label men for God
> And save them by the barrel load.

Religious education is clearly a far wider subject than religious instruction—which is only one of these five. It is concerned with all five and it can begin with any of them. Knowledge of the Bible, appreciation of the thrill of noble music, loyalty to the cause of Christ, helping a neighbour in difficulties, and

membership of a local Christian community are each of them
ways in which the Christian life can begin, although it is not,
so to speak, "full-orbed" until it is supplemented by the other
modes as well. There is also a question of emphasis. Different
people will emphasize different aspects of the faith according
to their temperament and gifts, but it should be a matter only
of emphasis and not of complete omission. The desire for the
same pattern of Christian life and faith for everybody does
violence not only to human nature but to the universal appeal
of the Gospel itself.

Who are to be the agents of religious education in this
wide sense? There are some who would restrict it entirely to
the professional clergy. There are some who out of suspicion
of denominationalism would leave it entirely in the hands of
the teacher. The truth is that no one agency can compass the
whole of it, yet neither can it be exactly apportioned to
different agencies. A school is not a church—it has a limited
age-range and it is concerned with many other matters besides
religion. It would appear, therefore, that instruction in the
Bible is the characteristic task of the school—of the Sunday
school always but also, in Great Britain, of the day school;
while in the United States and Canada it is the function of the
churches and their Directors of Religious Education. If we
say that cultivation of the emotional side of religion is the work
of the Church through its worship, we cannot deny that
the school assembly of a council school is often more
"worshipful" than the perfunctory type of worship which is
sometimes found in a church.

Then what of the extra-Church agencies? The Boy Scouts
and Girl Guides have put before young people moral and social
standards in ways often far more effective than the methods of
the Church, while the ritualistic side of those movements has
been a training of the emotions. Where, too, does the child's
home come in? In some homes all these various aspects of
Christian experience are present, in some none are present.
It seems, therefore, that so long as provision is made somewhere for each of these five modes of experience, it does not

really matter where or at what stage any one of them comes in.

There are, however, the child's own stages of development to be considered. With him there is a time for learning by heart, a time for joining a cause, a time for quiet and reflection, a time for stimulus, a time for action, a time for doctrine, a time for taking up responsibilities of church membership. These are matters for patience, understanding and adjustment. To seek after the right thing at the wrong time turns it into the wrong thing. To expect a child to use the language of the mature Christian is to produce a race of prigs, for a prig is a person whose attitude is out of keeping with his sensibility. And priggishness is the negation of Christian excellence.

CHAPTER II

SOME FALLACIES OF METHOD

RELIGIOUS education has been a wonderful playground for amateurs—using the word "amateur" in both senses, namely those who have no professional training and those who do it for the love of the work and feel that this is all that is required. It will be well, therefore, before coming to our main theme, to look at a number of popular theories—and practices—concerning religious education which still exist among us and each of which is inherently inadequate because it ignores the fundamental dilemma which we have just been considering. Both the hard-headed practical man and the earnest enthusiast are apt to fall down at this point, the one because he has "no use for theory" and the other because he is suspicious of anything that needs a hard intellectual training.

I will take five of these theories.

First, there is the view that by religious education we mean religious instruction and that alone.

An earlier generation was content to practise this belief by reading the Bible round in class and by rehearsing one's duty towards God and one's duty towards one's neighbour. Nowadays, with younger children we use projects and visual aids, and with older children we study much more the "background" of the Bible and of doctrine. But all these methods are apt to place a reliance upon knowledge as the chief (and often even as the only) thing needful in religious education.

The belief that knowledge *in itself* has some magical quality which affects character is a very ancient fallacy which arises from the "faculty" theory of psychology. The argument

C

runs somewhat like this: the mind is divided into faculties, and for the development of each faculty some particular intellectual exercise is necessary. Every subject has both form and content, and it is the form of the subject that provides exercise for this mental faculty. Latin, for instance, has a logical form. Mathematics is built up on reasoning. Science involves observation. Accordingly, if you put into the curriculum Latin, geometry and science you are providing training in accuracy, in reasoning and in observation.

This may possibly be true. But the argument then goes on to assume that the form of the subject is somehow *detachable* from its content, and hence each subject gives a mental training that is general and not just specific to the subject. Thus science trains in observation not only in the laboratory but everywhere—observation of the names of streets in a strange town, of people present in a room, of the details of an accident that one has witnessed. Latin gives a power of accuracy in analysing our feelings as well as in the use of the subjunctive mood. Mathematics enables one to reason dispassionately about politics as well as about triangles. In the same way the non-intellectual sides of school life are often justified because they too produce qualities of mind. Because football is impossible without the team spirit, it is assumed that to have compulsory football will of itself foster the team spirit in every walk of life. The prefect system has been justified on the quite unproven assumption that it trains children in a sense of responsibility which without any further stimulus will operate in later life when they are running a business or governing a colony. And learning the Bible or the creeds is believed by many people to have in itself the power to influence conduct, no matter what method of learning is pursued.

This belief in the alchemy of thought which transmutes the base metal of mere information into the gold of character is known in educational psychology under a variety of names. The theory is called "the transfer of training" or "formal training" or "mental discipline", and such investigations as have been made into it from the time of William James have shown it to be a fallacy. Specific training can give only specific results. If we want a general result we must adopt a general method to achieve it. To train a power of observation we have to require observation in all activities: we cannot rely on chemistry and physics to produce it for us. To train the team spirit in general is a different thing from training it in football alone.

Moreover, this theory as applied to Scripture has unexpected corollaries. It not only makes people content that their duty has been done as teachers and as Church members if they have provided for Scripture in the curriculum, but it also supplies a rough and ready test for teachers in those schools where religion is taken seriously. Religious jargon is as easy to acquire as any other: every denomination has its conventional terminology. Accordingly, boards of managers and other appointing bodies are often curiously satisfied if they can secure from a candidate assent in language which they understand, even though there is no guarantee that language represents reality. At no point in this arrangement is there any necessary connection with religion at all, and those who are content with it have confused conformity with conviction.

Is, then, the curriculum unimportant? By no means. It is important for two very sound reasons. In the first place the subject matter of our religion, the Old and New Testaments and the history of the Church, has what the educationists call "a high degree of correlation". That is to say, it links up a large number of subjects and interests, and enables them to interpret one another. On educational grounds alone any study which links geography, history and literature would be a most desirable subject in any curriculum, and this is what Scripture does. We shall have occasion to study this matter further in the next chapter.

But further, and more particularly: Christianity is a historical religion. It is concerned with events in time, and so there is in religious education a great deal that is factual, external and explicit and has to be learned.

Secondly, at the other extreme there is the point of view that religious education is a matter not of instruction but of what is called "atmosphere". This appears to be something altogether intangible and rarefied and non-intellectual. Apparently one recognizes it when it is present, but it cannot be described, and no one quite knows how it arrives.

This attitude to religion is adopted by two quite different and indeed opposed groups of people. They both take the line that religion is something emotional or irrational: but in one case it is because it transcends reason and is therefore superior to it; in the other, because it is more primitive than reason and is therefore inferior to it. Accordingly both of these extremists hold that religion cannot be taught as a school subject.

The argument is often continued to include an assumed respect for human personality which would forbid a man to thrust his own views upon others, and occasionally this is given a Scriptural turn from the text "The wind bloweth where it listeth". For a schoolmaster to step in with his mature experience and attempt to direct the spirit of God in some particular way, or to introduce a doctrine, or to seek to force a decision in these matters is held to do violence to the developing mind of another person, while to have examinations in such a subject is quite blasphemous. This is a point of view for which one can feel respect, but before noting its good points let us look at its fallacies.

In the first place Christianity, as has been said, is a historical faith, and the facts on which Christianity depends cannot be evolved from our own minds no matter how hard we try. The attempt might produce naturalism or quietism, but it cannot possibly produce anything that is specifically Christian.

In the second place, we may be sure that if Christians do not seek to educate people in Christianity there are other agencies that will educate them in other things. No such scruples about proselytizing ever assail humanists or scientists, or political parties, or business men. An equally definite

appeal, not always of a desirable kind, is made by the cinema
and popular literature. To imagine, therefore, that the child
will develop the Christian graces if we handicap Christian
influences while giving a clear field to those that are not
Christian, shows a very curious kind of loyalty to the highest
that one knows. A large-hearted charity towards error and a
coy silence towards truth is an inversion of the situation with
which Milton dealt in his *Areopagitica*.

But there is a still deeper fallacy in this position. The
view that a child's nature is somehow warped by any attempt
to inform it implies a conviction that we already know what a
child's nature is. This, of course, was Rousseau's attitude.
He believed that a person's nature was something quite
independent of circumstances or of education. It is also the
point of view of those who believe that by the age of eleven
it is known what a child's nature is, and he can then be
drafted into the type of school which will develop that
nature.

It seems to me that precisely the opposite is the case. It
is education that *reveals* a child's nature, and without education
no one could know what it is. The nature of a person is
discoverable, even to himself, only in his relationships to
situations, ideas and people that come his way, and if those
factors never appear it is impossible to tell what manner of
man he is. There have been people who all their lives imag-
ined that they liked jazz and that classical music was high-
brow, but who under the admirable wireless guidance of the
late Sir Walford Davies came to know that it is Beethoven
rather than "swing" that really speaks to their condition.

And in the case of religion it is even more so. It has been
contact with Christ that all down the ages has shown men
most truly what manner of men they are. There is, so to
speak, a diagnostic value in specific religious education which
no reliance on an amorphous atmosphere can ever give. And
this it possesses both for the giver and for the receiver. It
may be, therefore, that the shrinking from it is due not so
much to respect for other people's personality as to doubt

concerning one's own. To this extent religious education must always be different from other kinds of education—it makes a personal and not merely a professional demand upon the teacher. This demand is intrinsic in the nature of the subject, and it ought not to be confused with the different type of demand often made by some outside authority concerning a person's orthodoxy.

The emphasis on atmosphere does, however, remind us that what is hoped to arise out of religious education is a quality of life even more than an informed mind, and the second may quite easily get in the way of the first. When Thomas à Kempis declared "far rather had I feel a sorrow for my sin than know the definition of it", he was illustrating this distinction. Yet we may well ask ourselves how is a quality of life produced? Does it really come of itself? Is it so completely independent of outward form and circumstance and instruction? If it is thus unique we may despair of any attempt to produce it, for the deliberateness of the attempt will get in the way of every chance of success.

Inwardness and outwardness are not, however, so completely divorced. Inwardness, if not produced, is at any rate helped and disciplined by a right use of outwardness. We may consider here two influences that help this right use. The first is personal. "The soul of one lover is kindled by that of the other", says Augustine in a famous passage. Quality of life cannot be transmitted verbally: it comes by contact with people who already have it. This is what people mean when they utter the half-truth, "religion is caught not taught". Thus even your believer in "atmosphere" is not absolved from all effort in his hope that religion will somehow of itself develop in the hearts of those with whom he has to do. If he shirks the intellectual task he cannot avoid the moral and spiritual one. He must himself be the kind of person that he would wish others to be. For their sakes he must sanctify himself, whether or not he believes in religious instruction, or in what he would call preaching.

Furthermore, circumstances are of very great importance.

A right use of circumstances can produce a worshipful spirit, and a careless use can prevent it. Children may be untidy themselves, but they have a strong dislike of slovenliness in other people or in school. Things must be done decently and in order, whether it is the changing of classes, the organization of the time-table, the running of societies or the conduct of school assembly. The "atmosphere" of a community depends upon the smooth running of its organization— in the sense not of soul-less mechanical efficiency but rather of the perfect adaptation of means to ends. And for religious worship to have about it this feeling of eternal truth and rightness requires not less but more thought in its ordering.

It does not arrive accidentally. Beauty of form and colour and language, occasions of silence, careful choice of hymns and passages for reading (done not at the time but a long while before the time), an unhurried procedure even if the time allotted is short, all provide a setting which suggests the presence of God. Ritual is not something ecclesiastical— it is something psychological, a remembered and ordered way of doing things. Children are, moreover, very ritualistic. They like to know just where they come in, and nothing spoils a religious atmosphere for them more than a sense of uncertainty about the arrangements.

"Atmosphere", therefore, is the perfection of order, not its absence. In the same way it is the perfection of knowledge, not its absence. The absence of religious atmosphere may quite well be due to emptiness in religious thinking, and the way to produce it is not to turn away from the intellectual side of religion but to cultivate it with greater wisdom and thoroughness.

Thirdly, there is the view that all that matters is the personality of the teacher.

It is obvious, therefore, that religious education requires "the right kind of people" for its accomplishment. Once, however, we place our reliance on personality the question arises concerning standards of suitability.

First of all, what do we mean by "suitable people"? It clearly means people who know their subject, who have a thorough acquaintance with the Scriptures and can teach intelligently. The standard of knowledge and of ability ought not to be lower in this subject than in the teaching of history or science. Yet we know not only that the standard is usually lower but also that it is far too often assumed that a compensation for this can be found in the excellence of character of the teacher. In English secondary schools the difficulty is increased because teachers of all other subjects have a degree in the subject which they teach, so that they can be assumed at any rate to possess the content of their subject. In Scripture, however, very few indeed possess any qualification at all equivalent to a degree in history or mathematics. On the other hand, people with a theological degree and a thorough understanding of the content of Scripture are often in the same position as other specialists—unable to mediate it to immature minds. The specialist, moreover, is often quite at a loss to make any distinction between children at different ages in their attitude to the subject.

The place of doctrine also creates a difficulty. To make the test of suitability doctrinal "soundness" (whatever that may mean) often results in a doctrinal approach to children *at all ages*. There are people who cannot teach the story of the deliverance of the Israelites from Egypt without drawing from it lessons of doctrinal significance, and a favourite way of avoiding the (superficial) difficulties in the stories of Cain and Abel, or Jacob, or David, is to treat these stories simply as pegs on which to hang doctrine, or by allegorizing to allow ignorance to masquerade as reverence. Its condemnation lies in the fact that it recognizes no line of development in the young mind, and no parallel between the growth of the sense of God in the human heart and its growth in the course of history. The first duty of any teacher of Scripture is to deal with it in its own context rather than to read into it doctrinal or any other ideas of his own.

"Suitability", therefore, involves both knowledge of subject matter and ability to teach it.

But two further demands are often made upon teachers of this subject. The first is that they must believe what they teach, and the second that they must practise what they believe.

What do we mean by "believing what you teach"? How, for example, would a Catholic teacher of history in a school mainly Protestant be expected to handle the subject of the dissolution of the monasteries? Could he be unbiased, and if not, ought he to be replaced for the time being by someone who shares the orthodox Protestant view? What sort of scientific scholarship would result if you turned loose in a biology lesson an old-fashioned fundamentalist who thought evolution was of the devil, or if you had for your geology lesson a man who believed that the world was created in six days? And so we might go on. "Suitability" and "believing what you teach" might appear to require a large staff of teachers minutely classified according to their personal agreement with the subject matter.

There are two ways out. Either you impose a test on the teacher to insure that his views agree with yours on every controversial religious subject—which, of course, is the method in Catholic and some other denominational schools— or you assure yourself that the teacher is an honest gentleman who will not misuse his position by substituting proselytism for teaching. The second is surely the only one in keeping with the idea of education. If the teacher has a point of view of his own (and he would be a poor teacher if he had not) he will nevertheless make clear that there are other points of view also and he will in all fairness let his pupils know what they are. And he will have an attitude of respect to the subject matter. It has been built up in the course of generations by thinking men and so he will be chary of handing out slap-dash judgements of "right" and "wrong".

Milton was not "wrong" because he took literally the early chapters of Genesis, nor is a man necessarily "right" because he has grasped the document theory of the Pentateuch. The ability to appreciate a person or a subject in itself apart from any emotional concern it may have for oneself is one mark of the truly educated man. When James Maxton, the crusading Scottish Socialist M.P., died, the man who broadcast the public appreciation of his life work was Walter Elliot, a prominent leader of the Conservative Party. Belief in a subject and suitability to teach it are concerned with selflessness and good manners even more than with personal party allegiance, and this attitude in a teacher is infinitely to be preferred to an uncritical or an intolerant orthodoxy. With this attitude a good teacher *always* "believes what he teaches", and if he did not, he would not be teaching it.

But what do we mean by the further demand often made on a teacher of Scripture that he should "practise what he believes"? Many people are, no doubt, content to interpret this as meaning membership of a church, or facility to express one's beliefs in accepted language, or the observance of certain taboos or commandments. There is an unwillingness to accept even excellence of character as a qualification unless that excellence is deliberately linked up with some outward religious profession. Yet if religion is to any extent caught rather than taught, it can come only through personal influence, and orthodoxy in these matters unaccompanied by the religious temper is as likely to influence people in the contrary direction as in the way intended.

Fourthly, underneath all these difficulties lies the question of control. The Church wishes to control the teachers and to safeguard the position of religion in the schools. The teachers feel that they should be the judges of professional competence in this as in all other such matters. The Education Authorities wish to have all education in their hands and they look upon Church control as a nuisance and an anachronism. In these days in Britain the controversy over control is at the root of the problem.

The continued existence of denominational schools along-side the schools of the nation is often defended on the ground that this safeguards religion.[1] Here it is not merely a matter of curriculum or of teachers: it is an assumption that the mere possession of schools by a Church promotes religious educa-tion. From what we have already seen it is clear that this conclusion is by no means certain. The most that can be said (and it may be the ultimate justification for keeping denom-inational schools) is that such control gives the opportunity for well-concerned and intelligent people to make religious education a success. Yet, today in Britain, with State-controlled schools increasing in number, we have passed away from the position that Church schools are Christian schools and Council schools are non-Christian: both types of school get recruits for their staff from precisely the same sources, and a man does not shed his religion nor assume it according as his post is in a Council or in a Church school.

This question of control reaches out still farther. All over Africa and India there are denominational schools run by European and American missionary societies, and the question of religious education is an acute anxiety. Even the Free Churches of England, which are on the whole strongly opposed to denominational schools in the mother country, are defenders of such schools on the mission field and upholders of the grants-in-aid system. In Africa, however, I have noticed how easily satisfied some missions are with the conditions which they believe to be necessary for religious education. They are so apt to believe that missionary control *of itself* ensures what they want that they are relatively in-attentive to any other requirement. Again and again, how-ever, both at home and abroad we come back to the truth that in education there is no machine discoverable which will of itself do the work that can be done only by a person. This is true whether that machine be an organization, or a time-table or an agreed syllabus of religious instruction.

[1] This refers particularly to the schools in Britain. The situation in North America and on the Continent is different.

In denominational schools the clergy or ministers of the denomination have, of course, right of entry. But what are we to do about schools that do not belong to the churches?

Religion is still associated in the minds of a great many persons with deep and unfathomable mysteries with which only the clergy can deal. This may be so in the long run, but *as far as the school is concerned* it is obviously nonsense. The clergy are no longer monopolists in religious knowledge, nor indeed do they for the most part claim to be such. Very few of them have had that kind of teaching experience which enables them to deal with children of different grades and mediate to them the knowledge which they themselves possess. Yet the claim is frequently made that the clergy should come into the schools to teach doctrine as well as "Scripture", or, alternatively, that the children should leave the school for the church during school hours for instruction in religion—right of entry or right of exit!

The difficulty about this is that it divorces a man from his office, and in the matter of religious education it is all too easy to hold that with teachers it is the man that matters and with clergy it is the office. Those who wish to be very strict about the orthodoxy and the churchmanship of teachers before they are allowed to give religious instruction often raise no question at all in the case of the clergy. But surely it is absurd to assume that a man becomes competent to educate people simply through the mechanics of ordination, and we cannot assume that the ability to train children, even in worship, is something automatically acquired as a kind of by-product of a theological course. The simplicity of a little child comes naturally to a little child, but the understanding of that simplicity by an adult (a vitally important matter in teaching) is either a Heaven-sent gift which very few people, particularly men, possess, or it is the product of painstaking effort and study which not many people are willing to undergo. And so before we accept the principle of right of entry for the clergy into the nation's schools it is not irrelevant to require that they should be at least as competent to teach religious knowledge as the teacher is expected to be to teach other kinds of knowledge.

Fifthly, the question of control goes deeper, however, than even the ownership of buildings or the supervision of religious teaching.

It is held in some quarters that no real Christian instruction is possible if the teaching given is not intimately linked up with an actually existing, living, worshipping Christian community, and this is one reason why Church people have felt compelled to defend denominational schools.

This view is a good indication of the truth that Christianity is a great deal more than religious knowledge or ethics. There is a certain type of moralist who would quite approve of religious teaching in schools on the ground that it is good for character, and that if we only lived up to the Sermon on the Mount what a much better world this would be. Jesus is ranked with Socrates and other great teachers, although above them all in personal character, and therefore the study of his life and times has a moralizing effect upon the spirit of man. The Old Testament is useful because it shows how and how far men have transcended the cruder levels of morality, and also because it provides the background for the life of Christ. Moreover, this whole story has come down to English people enshrined in the stately language of the Authorized Version, which in itself is an appeal to the right kind of emotions.

This position is quite sound as far as it goes, but it is not Christianity. The Christian view is concerned not with what man has done but with what God has done. "He commended his love toward us in that while we were yet sinners Christ died for the ungodly." This, to the plain man, may be nonsense or else simply Paul's rationalizing of his own experience, but it is not the plain man who is the judge of these things—it is the redeemed man or the converted man. Spiritual things can only be spiritually discerned, and in religion we are dealing with spiritual things.

Moreover, it is an entire mistake to assume that Christian ethics are separable from the task of following Christ. When the plain man commends the Sermon on the Mount "if only" it were practicable, it is precisely the qualification "if only" that marks the difference between Christian ethics and other standards of conduct. Rightly or wrongly it is the Christian conviction that Christian ethics spring out of and *only* out of a living fellowship with Christ, and in that union the Sermon on the Mount is perfectly practicable.

The highest expression of that fellowship is to be found not in conduct at all but in worship. And worship is not simply bowing down to someone whom we acknowledge to be higher than ourselves; it is belonging to a community created by Him and through which He is made known by name to the world of men. It is, therefore, an *activity* and is rightly called "service".

Worship can be carried on by anybody who is worshipful and who is sufficiently representative of the community. This, I imagine, is why in school it is more suitable for the Head of the school to conduct it rather than an assistant or even a chaplain. But as an expression of Christian faith worship in its fullest sense is clearly an act of the Church. It is part of the institutional side of Christianity and not merely a method of playing upon the emotions of children—even if this is done wisely. It is the society rather than the individual that is responsible for carrying it on from age to age, and it requires adoption into the society rather than the mere copying of externals in order to give it its full meaning. I suppose it would be possible for anyone acquainted with masonic ritual to stage a masonic celebration; it might be beautiful and indeed impressive; but apart from connection with a Lodge of Freemasons it would lose its real point. Christian worship has the same quality, and as it is the source and inspiration of Christian ethics, the Christian community is in the last resort the factor that gives meaning and effect to ethics as well as to worship.

Nevertheless there are certain considerations that ought

not to be forgotten. In the first place Christianity has propagated itself in two ways—one is through personal conviction, the other is by the spread of Christian ideals; and both ways are important. Adding to the number of convinced Christians is the direct method, and without it the method of diffusion would not be available at all. But given the existence of a convinced core of believers, there arises an influence which permeates other people who are not convinced believers at all and may even be antagonistic to the Church as an institution. And diffused Christianity has gradually influenced the penal code, the relations between capital and labour, the position of women, the education of children and indeed every aspect of life. It may not be the business of the school to aim at church membership, but it is certainly concerned with this diffusion of Christian principles.

In the second place, it is easy to underestimate the value of the school itself as a community. If the work of the school is to be permeated with the Christian spirit, and if religious education is of such great importance, the school must surely have a character of its own and be itself a kind of Christian community. For it to be merely an appendage to the Church—which nowadays means not the undivided, visible Church, but a denomination or even a single congregation—is to limit rather than to enlarge its religious usefulness. Moreover, denominationalism is one reason why the teachers who are keenest on religious education so often resent the intrusion of the Churches into their work. They have been trying to build up a corporate religious spirit in the school, and by reason of the agitation of outsiders that unity has to be broken up and some children sent off to one church and some to another. How can the school function properly in this regard if it is wilfully split up into factions in which the children themselves have no interest?

The school, however, is a special kind of community, and in certain ways it can and does preserve Christian values better than the local church. It is, no doubt, a limited community; unlike the Church, which includes all age ranges, it is composed of a small age range; and most schools are for one sex only—although over against this is to be placed the greater place of women in the world of school than in the Church. Nevertheless, within its limits it constitutes a world in which ideals can not only be sought after but also become practical; right can triumph and wrong be worsted in a school society more surely than in the world outside, and the consequences of one's action are the more readily visible.

The school affords a field of experiment which the world outside does not afford, and therefore the school has the possibility of being in embryo a Christian Society—a possibility which the Church in these days has lost. Of this society the act of Christian worship can be the most appropriate expression. The school has its tradition of learning: more than any other society it is the guardian of the heritage of the ages; all races and nations and epochs have brought their contribution into it; it is a closely knit body in itself and yet it is connected with the world outside through the parent, the teacher and the rate-payers, so that it is necessarily concerned with the service of the future as well as with the treasures of the past.

A community of this sort in a country such as Britain or Australia or America is inevitably a centre of diffused Christianity. If it is informed by these principles it is doing a noble work, and the business of the clergy as well as other Christian folk should be to help it to fulfil its own function rather than to give it a function which is alien to it.

CHAPTER III

THE BIBLE IN EDUCATION

I

THE roots of Christianity are in the Bible, for Christianity is concerned with events and those events are recorded in the Bible.

But this association with events is a *concern* and not just a connection. That the Israelites came out of Egypt, that Amos prophesied in 753 B.C., that the people of Judah went into exile in Babylon, that Jesus Christ was born in Palestine in the time of Augustus and was crucified about the year A.D. 28, are all historical events of the same factual nature as the flight of Mohammed or the events leading to the American Revolution. If Christianity were historical in no other sense than this it would be on a level with Buddhism or Islam, which also had a historical origin. But it is *concerned* about its origin in a very special way. Like Judaism it is rooted in events of more than ordinary significance, for these events were interpreted in subsequent ages as proofs not only of the existence of God but also of his very special relationship with the people to whom these events happened. 861763

The Old Testament event was the deliverance from Egypt.

I am the Lord thy God which brought thee up out of the land of Egypt and out of the house of bondage

is the refrain that runs through the whole of the Old Testament. This was a historical event but it was also the basic fact of the Hebrew faith. Because of this great event and the events which immediately flowed from it the Hebrews were bound together with God in a partnership of mutual obligation, the like of which no other nation of antiquity had ever achieved. This partnership, or "covenant", was the basis of the appeal of the Hebrew spiritual leaders to their wayward people. It was like a marriage relationship, and any deviation from it, any running after other gods, was branded by the prophets as "whoredom" and unfaithfulness.

The New Testament events were the Crucifixion under Pontius Pilate of Jesus of Nazareth and His subsequent resurrection from the dead. Here, too, is a blend of history and faith. Tacitus and Josephus are supporting authorities for the Crucifixion, but the actual physical resurrection was witnessed by no one. It was attested after the event only by those who were specially committed in loyalty to Jesus, and its truth depends on the testimony of those who by what they called the power of the risen Christ were altogether changed in their attitude to God and to one another. Of these the chief witness was the Apostle Paul, who had never seen Jesus in the flesh at all. But the risen Christ did not appear to Pilate or Caiaphas or the Jerusalem mob. He was no longer seen in the streets or in the temple. Only where two or three were gathered together in His name was He in the midst of them. And so it has continued unto this day.

In Christianity, therefore, the basic events had a significance wider than those of Judaism. They were not merely historical beginnings of the faith: they were also the historical pattern of a continued experience.

2

This, then, is where we begin in our education in the Christian faith. And I suggest that we begin with the Bible as we have it in English.

In three notable lectures "On Reading the Bible" and in another on "The Capital Difficulty of Prose", Sir Arthur Quiller-Couch, professor of English literature, poet and novelist, brings us back to the glories of the English version.

I grant you that the forty-seven men who produced the Authorized Version worked in the main upon Tyndale's version, taking that for their basis . . . But when Tyndale has been granted you have yet to face the miracle that forty-seven men—not one of them known, outside of this performance, for any superlative talent—sat in committee and almost consistently, over a vast extent of work— improved upon what Genius had done. I give you the word of an old committee man that this is not the way of committees . . .

and after quoting one or two well-known sentences, he continues

When a nation has achieved this manner of diction, these rhythms for its dearest beliefs, a literature is surely established. . . . It has cadences, holy and sublime, yet so harmonizes them that the voice is always one. Simple men—holy and humble men of heart like Izaak Walton or Bunyan—have their lips touched and speak to the homelier tune. Proud men, scholars—Milton, Sir Thomas Browne—practise the rolling Latin sentence: but upon the rhythms of our Bible they, too, fall back . . . The Bible controls its enemy Gibbon as surely as it haunts the curious music of a light sentence of Thackeray's. It is in everything we see, hear, feel, because it is in us, in our blood.[1]

This is a good start and we shall seek to make our pupils acquainted with the text of the English Bible. It will come as a surprise to them, no doubt, to discover that already they use it familiarly, without knowing it. The football team, they will say, smote their rivals hip and thigh, partly because the opposing captain had played the fool and hadn't time to set his house in order, and they will not realize that in this short sentence they have quoted the Bible three times. I doubt whether it is possible fully to appreciate the wit of Mr. P. G. Wodehouse without a good knowledge of the English Bible, and of course any serious sustained writing is almost bound to use phrases that come from the Authorized Version.

[1] *The Art of Writing*. Lecture vi.

For English-speaking people the Bible as a monument of English justifies its place in any scheme of education. The word "numinous" has recently acquired some vogue among us as a shorthand way of expressing Wordsworth's

> sense sublime
> Of something far more deeply interfused,
> Whose dwelling is the light of setting suns,
> And the round ocean and the living air,
> And the blue sky, and in the mind of man.

Well, the Bible is "numinous" but in a still deeper and more intimate sense than that attained by Wordsworth. It has a name for this "something" and it is the record of His dealings with mankind in the history of the most interesting people of antiquity. We shall consider this side of the matter shortly.

But the Bible is also numinous in its very language. This is so in the Greek and still more in the Hebrew, but the English reader has it also in his own mother tongue.

> Behold a king shall reign in righteousness and princes shall rule in judgement. And a man shall be as an hiding place from the wind, and a covert from the tempest, as rivers of water in a dry place, as the shadow of a great rock in a weary land.

This is a word of prophecy. But the historians can do it equally well:

> And he said unto him Went not mine heart with thee when the man turned again from his chariot to meet thee? Is it a time to receive money and to receive garments and oliveyards and vineyards and sheep and oxen and men-servants and maidservants? The leprosy therefore of Naaman shall cleave unto thee and unto thy seed for ever. And he went out from his presence a leper as white as snow.

The New Testament writers dealing with a much less picturesque language than the Hebrew nevertheless capture the same terse rhythm which comes through into the English. Attempt to tell the story of the Prodigal Son in fewer

words than Luke employs in Chapter xv and you will find
that it cannot be done. And yet it is all there, no excess and
no defect, just the right words for the right effect. And
although the Greek of St. Paul almost defeated Tyndale and
nowadays we need a modern translation for the understanding
of it, what more numinous passage in English could you
find than this—

> For which cause we faint not: but though our out-
> ward man perish yet our inward *man* is renewed day by
> day. For our light affliction which is but for a moment
> worketh for us a far more exceeding *and* eternal weight
> of glory?

I have italicized the words that those honest forty-seven men
italicized although there was no real need for it. They would
not have it thought, however, that they had interfered by
one jot or tittle with the sacred text, and so they owned up
to the addition of words which the scrupulous reader might
not be able to find in exact equivalent in the original.

I am not one of those who on principle abhor modern
versions. There has been considerable progress in Hebrew
and Greek scholarship since 1611. There are gross mistakes
in the King James's Version which a better knowledge of
the original could not but alter. "Thou hast multiplied
the nation," says Isaiah, "and *not* increased the joy: they
joy before thee according to the joy in harvest." Clearly
something has gone wrong here and the English Revised
Version puts it right by leaving out the word "not". And
there are many other examples of like nature. Our Lord,
Paul writes to the Philippians, "thought it not robbery to be
equal with God". The noun here is used really in the
passive sense and has misled the forty-seven. Later versions
have corrected it.

We shall find it necessary, no doubt, from time to time
to use other translations, particularly the American Standard
Version and also J. B. Phillips (his *Letters to Younger Churches*
most certainly, if we are to give the adults and adolescents
any enthusiasm for Paul's Epistles), and perhaps a few more.

But all this is for the understanding of the text. They do not rule out the Authorized (King James's) Version.

It is worth noticing that the forty-seven did not use the language of their own day—they went back to the even statelier model of 1526 and it is nice to know, although not important, that 90 per cent. of their words are of Saxon origin while Shakespeare comes a close second with 85. The Lord's Prayer in its usual form has 65 words, and 59 of them are Saxon. When you wish to express yourself you take the handiest words for the purpose, whatever their origin, but words with the longest pedigree are usually found to express those experiences that are deepest and most universal. And perhaps because of this the very phraseology of the English Bible easily slips into the vocabulary of simple and uneducated Christian men.

One such—a shepherd—I heard pray in a moorland chapel in Yorkshire: "If thou hadst dealt with us after our sins or rewarded us according to our iniquities we should not have been in thy house tonight pleading with Thee." Have I used the word "uneducated"? I take it back. No man who could extemporize in language such as that could ever be called uneducated. He was one of those of whom it was written "He hath made us kings and priests unto God". Professor Thomas Henry Huxley (an unexpected Saul among the prophets) had such men in mind in his great panegyric on the Bible, when, after bidding us consider that "this book has been woven into the life of all that is best and noblest in English history", he concludes

and finally, that it forbids the veriest hind who never left his village, to be ignorant of the existence of other countries and other civilizations, and of a great past, stretching back to the furthest limits of the oldest nations in the world. By the study of what other book could children be so much humanized and made to feel that each figure in that vast historical procession fills, like themselves, but a momentary space in the interval between two eternities, and earns the blessings or the curses of all

time, according to its effort to do good and hate evil,
even as they also are earning their payment for their
work?[1]

There is "numinous" for you!

3

We shall therefore get our children to read the Bible and
hear it read—*well* read, none of this reading round the class,
a verse apiece, as they used to do. There is music in this
language and music for its expression requires a musician,
somebody trained and experienced in the job. If school
worship does nothing more than accustom the children to
hearing the Bible well read they have staked their claim to
their own native heritage.

And with that there is learning by heart—yes, even when
they do not understand what it is all about. For it is music,
remember, and music can be enjoyed and hummed and
recalled even when the words (if any) are not understood and
the structure is a deep mystery. Moreover, learning by heart
has to be done when it is easy to do it. There is a time for
everything under the sun and there is a time for learning by
heart. It is difficult later in life, but a child who grows up
with these cadences in his possession has a mind endowed with
all the grace of ancestry. A young person of this sort, aged
seven, who without effort, simply by hearing them frequently
read, had become permanently possessed of several parables of
Jesus, Isaiah xi and xxxv and a few more well-known passages,
was found on a rainy day looking through the window at a
badly drained lawn and repeating to herself over and over
again

And the parched ground shall become a pool and
the thirsty land springs of water.

Here was the prophecy being fulfilled before her very eyes!

[1] Collected Essays, vol. 3. "Science and Education", pp. 397-8.

But the words had been learned long before, at a time when there was no indication of their relevance.

Naturally, therefore, the Bible contains admirable material for children both to learn and to understand. The Arthurian cycle has no points of superiority for young children over the Joseph cycle and still less over the later cycles of Elijah and Elisha stories. These came into existence in much the same way as the stories of Arthur, and if you want later examples of the same process you can find them by the shoal in the *Gesta Romanorum*. To children they are all stories, and that is as it should be. Let them get hold of them and know them, not bowdlerized nor "adapted for the young" but as they are, in their own incomparable mother tongue. For perfect simplicity of diction and narrative style let the stories of Isaac and Rebekah and of Naaman stand as examples. Gideon and Samson are not too bloodthirsty for young lads who, in any case, listen-in to worse stuff on the radio and see far worse at the pictures. And of course the parables of our Lord have always been among the world's best stories for children.

Much of this material will raise problems. What had poor Cain done that God refused his offering? Wasn't Elijah a kind of Bluebeard for slaughtering all those misguided priests of Baal? Problems arise with anything told to children—*their* problems, not always ours, and not always where we most expect them. Well, there has to be a short answer suited to their age. The full meaning will come later.

The reference to Quiller-Couch recalls the services he rendered to the teaching of the Bible in the schools of England. In the lecture on "The Capital Difficulty of Prose" delivered in 1913 he asked his Cambridge audience

> Does it or does it not strike you as queer that the people who set you "courses of study" in English Literature never include the Authorized Version, which not only intrinsically but also historically is out and away the greatest book of English Prose?

This was queer not only in the universities but also in the

schools of the nation. The schools, however, were labouring under a disability imposed by a false educational theory. They could give religious instruction, but in schools not belonging to churches there was no guarantee that it would be given by people able and willing to do so. The Scripture lesson was normally first in the day's time-table, so that *all* teachers in the school, of whatever competence or willingness, were occupied with it. Moreover, in the training colleges, even those belonging to churches, Scripture was only an "additional option" in the college course, so that students who took it handicapped themselves with an extra subject not recognized in their certificate. Consequently not many students were willing to take the risk. Underlying both these factors was the familiar theory that Scripture, *however taught*, was magically transmuted into good conduct and Christian living.

The Scripture lesson, therefore, was not very hopeful ground for experiment. So Quiller-Couch turned to the English lesson. In a series called *The King's Treasuries*, very much used in schools, he saw to it that an anthology of the Authorized Version appeared as an item and that in other general anthologies the English Bible had its place. By 1924 interest aroused in the English lesson had spilled over into the Scripture lesson, and the historical method had sufficiently proved itself as the only educational treatment of the subject. In that year, therefore, the County Council of Cambridgeshire was moved to make an experiment and to produce for its schools an Agreed Syllabus of Religious Instruction. It was agreed upon by the Church of England, the Free Churches, the teachers and the Local Education Authority. It was interesting that in the discussions on the syllabus the dividing lines of opinion hardly ever coincided with the representative nature of the members. They were always cross divisions—an indication of how little the denominational issue affected the position.

This syllabus was a pioneer in the field and it has had two drastic revisions in late years. At first it followed the lead of theological professors whose angle of approach was that of the latest expert scholarship. Gradually it has passed more into the hands of the teachers who see the subject from the point of view of class-room teaching. These are the "middle men" who are so badly needed in the teaching of the Bible— men and women who can follow what the scholars are doing but who can mediate this expert knowledge to the needs and understanding of the young. There are such people in the oldest subjects like classics, science or history, but this intermediate class does not as yet exist in any large numbers in the teaching of the Bible.

The Education Act of 1944 was followed by administrative provisions which swept away the two disabilities I have mentioned. Scripture can now be taught at any period of the day. Not all teachers have to do it, and so the way is cleared for people who have had training and wish to teach it. More-over, the subject is now part of the teacher's certificate, on a level with other subjects. Consequently the colleges are setting themselves to provide proper instruction for the future teachers. Meanwhile the Local Authorities are seeking to underpin the position by summer schools and courses of lectures for the enthusiastic amateurs who have not had the opportunity for this specialist training.

The Cambridgeshire syllabus has been followed by others. Any Local Education Authority can prescribe any syllabus for use in its schools, and those of Cambridgeshire, Sunderland, London, the West Riding and Durham are among the most popular. But local territorial loyalty has been provoked by these new opportunities and Authorities like to produce their own syllabuses. Consequently there are now in operation in England nearly forty of these agreed syllabuses.

4

And now for the Bible itself.

One blessed word which continually recurs in discussions on teaching is the word "correlation". I have already used it myself (page 21). What it means is the linking up of one subject with another. The value of this proceeding is that it joins together that which should never have been put asunder, namely the various aspects of life and work and the heritage from the past. To see life as a whole is as necessary as to see it in bits—indeed more necessary. Subjects, therefore, which have about them this quality of wholeness are more to be preferred in the curriculum than those which are specialisms and nothing else. Biology, for instance, is a good subject for this purpose. It links up with physiology, hygiene, geography and economics. History is another. You can have history of anything—not only kings and queens, battles, murder and sudden death but clothes, houses, farming, religion, literature and painting.

Now the Bible has a high correlation value, especially now that we accept the historical method—of which more shortly. Indeed, I know of no subject of higher value in this regard. It correlates history, geography, literature and religion—which is just another way of saying that it views the life of man in all its aspects—in relation to the natural world, the past, the present, the future, and to the world of unseen and timeless reality.

Let us look at these in turn.

First of all, with regard to geography. You can learn from Professor Fleure in an excellent series of books romantically called *Corridors of Time* that one of the fundamental considerations to keep in mind in the study of human life is the contrast between the desert and the fertile land, or, as he calls it, "the steppe and the sown". There is a constant clash between these two types of civilization. You find it to this day in unexpected places such as Eastern Nigeria, where the pastoral tribes and the farming and industrial community represent contrasting and often conflicting ways of life. Miss Mildred Cable found it in the Gobi Desert.[1] It is indeed found everywhere. The desert dweller has no abiding city, he moves with his flocks from one pasture ground to another, he has no real estate, no property except his tent and his herds. And he has no

[1] M. Cable and F. French: *The Gobi Desert*, p. 157.

neighbours. At night he sleeps under the open heaven and the whole arch of the sky looks down upon him. His is a hard life with few comforts, and it makes for austerity, self-denial and equality. The desert is the home of monotheism, often of a fanatical kind. God is One in the desert and there is no other except demons. (You will find a mention of some of these in Isaiah xxxiv. 14. R.V. margin.) He is made known to men in the starry sphere and in the great silences and in the heart of man.

The sown land produces a different type. He plants his crops and has to wait till they come up. This calls for a more permanent dwelling than a tent. He builds a house, and other men build theirs near to him. Soon a community springs into being, and a class of men appears who are not themselves primary producers but who serve the producers as merchants and as craftsmen. In a community the natural divisions of mankind—wise and foolish, strong and weak, practical and theoretical—become the basis of a social order. The strong exploit the weak and the wise take advantage of the unwise. Class divisions appear, oppression and tyranny raise their heads, and sin becomes socialized as well as individual. In primitive agrarian communities of this sort every field and bush, every stone and high hill has its religious significance. The dependence of men on the fertility of nature draws attention to human fertility, and religion has a strong sexual bias. The multitude of gods of the fertile land and, what is more important, of goddesses, also makes of religion something warm, friendly, domestic and corrupt.

Now let us look at the Bible in this light. Is not this the meaning of the Cain and Abel myth? Here you have the pastoral and the agricultural in conflict, and the later writer who handles this myth and incorporates it into the history of his country represents the prophetic distaste for the settled life of the town. Cain, you will remember, "builded a city" and the prophetic writers were always suspicious of that kind of activity. Here then at the very opening of the Bible is this age-long cleavage between the steppe and the sown. Look

at Amos—the first two chapters. Here are all Israel's neighbours up for judgement—Damascus, Gaza, Tyre, Edom,
Ammon, Moab and Judah—and what is it that Amos hates
most? In every judgement there occurs the word "palaces".
"I will send a fire on the wall of Gaza and it shall devour the
palaces thereof." There is no mistaking it. The settled
community has divided into strong and weak, the strong have
taken possession and exploited the weak and the symbol of
their tyranny is the palace. And Amos himself was a desert
dweller, an inhabitant of the wilderness of Tekoah.

The contrast is seen throughout the Old Testament. If you
wanted to find God you would more likely find Him in the
desert than among the townsfolk. And the same theme occurs
in the New Testament. When Jesus seeks to study God's will
for Himself he goes into the wilderness. There the conflict
between God and Satan takes on a simple form, unclouded by
the prudential considerations of society outside. When
Paul is converted he goes down into Arabia—(Galatians i.
17). Jesus takes His disciples into a desert place when He
wishes to instruct them. The tremendous curse upon Rome
in the Revelation xviii concludes its catalogue of the merchan-
dise of a busy, luxurious and tyrannical city with the item "and
souls of men". It was the belief of all the Biblical writers
that souls of men were in direst danger in those places where
men flocked together in communities.

5

Secondly, let us consider the correlation of the Bible with
literature.

Far too much has been made of the easy distinction between
"the Bible as literature" and "the devotional use of the
Bible". Too often it means that the historical view of the
Bible is one thing but that you have to forget all about that
when you come to your devotions. With many people,
therefore, the devotional use of the Bible means harking back
to the old fundamentalist theory and using a Biblical verse as

a peg on which to hang all sorts of ideas that may come into your mind when you are being devotional. Even a great book like William Temple's *Readings in St. John's Gospel* does not wholly escape from this attitude.

In dealing with literature, unless you are a mere philologer, the important questions to ask are: What is the man trying to say, has he said it, and was it worth saying? In Milton's *Paradise Lost* I am faced with a view of the universe which is out of date and misleading. Nevertheless the theme of the origin and punishment of sin is immensely worth while and given the limitations of the age in which he lived Milton dealt with it in the grand manner and with a highly "numinous" quality. Form and content need to be welded into one in order to make great literature. And if this is true of structure it is no less true of appreciation. Unless we appreciate the value and importance of what a man is trying to say our criticism of how he says it is mere scholasticism. When, for instance, Mr. F. R. Leavis, of Cambridge, doing homage at the shrine of Mr. T. S. Eliot, says that "Milton's dislodgement in the past decade, after his two centuries of predominance, was effected with remarkably little fuss" he tells us more about F. R. Leavis and about T. S. Eliot's "Catholic" prejudices than about Milton.[1]

What, then, is the Bible trying to say and how does it say it? It is a book of religion and if a man has no use for religion he will clearly not appreciate the Bible. He will let himself be put off with the crude anthropomorphisms of the book of Genesis and the apparently meaningless word-spinnings of St. Paul. He will miss the real genius of Bunyan's *Pilgrim's Progress* for the same reason. Like Mr. Fred Hoyle he will gleefully controvert Job xix. 26 without once asking himself if the Authorized Version gives the exact sense of the Hebrew original. Surely if a work of literature is concerned with the deeper experiences of humanity we must bring to it at any rate a mind of a somewhat similar character whether we are

[1] See for an admirable treatment of this thesis Logan Pearsall Smith's *Milton and His Modern Critics*.

Christian believers or not, and this is as true of the appreciation of Browning or Tennyson's *In Memoriam* or Sir Thomas
Browne or the Greek tragedians as it is of the Bible. Robert
Lynd, that charming literary critic, once said that no one could
appreciate Shakespeare's tragedies who had not a sense of
the sinfulness of sin, and this is a sound literary as well as a
moral judgement.

We have already noticed something about the language of
the English Bible. But there are notable literary features of
the Bible itself. There is, for instance, its superb narrative
style. What could be better done than the story of Naaman
already mentioned, or the graphic account of the mystery of
Sennacherib? Byron's "the Assyrian came down like a wolf
on the fold" is overloaded with metaphor. Compare it with
the account of the same event in II Kings xix or Isaiah xxxvii,
where there is hardly a redundant word. "And when men
arose early in the morning, behold they were all dead
corpses." Byron takes longer to say this and is much less
effective.

The New Testament narrative has the same qualities. The
story of Paul's voyage and shipwreck in Acts xxvii is narrative
at its best, but I would call your attention still more to the
accounts of the Crucifixion. For economy of words, absence
of all comment, plain objective reporting, terrible in its
effect by reason of its very austerity, there is no better prose
writing of the kind anywhere.

But narrative is not the only form. There is the short
story like the book of Ruth, the point of which does not
appear until the last sentence and even the last word; drama
like the story of Saul and David or the book of Job; the
treatise, although in this case a misguided one, like the book
of Ecclesiastes; the novel, although in this case not a religious
one, such as the book of Esther; pamphlet literature of an
early "resistance movement" like Daniel; poetry, not only
Psalms and *Proverbs* but also in the histories and the prophetic
books; and a unique sermon literature in the prophets. And
throughout the whole *corpus* the theme is the same—God's

relation to man and man's relation to God. Sometimes the writer gropes in the dark as in Job and Psalm lxxiii. Sometimes he misses fire altogether as in Judges v. Sometimes he is gloriously assured as in Isaiah xl to lv. But whatever he writes this is his theme.

And now let us try a little comparison of the Bible with other writers on similar themes.

You will remember that horrible story of the Athenian massacre of the friendly people of the little island of Melos in 416 B.C. Thucydides was so shocked by it that he expounds at length the discussion between the helpless Melians and their Athenian enemies. Euripides was more than shocked: he was outraged, and he produced a play on the theme, but setting it for convention's sake in the old legend of Troy. *The Trojan Woman* is almost unbearable in its pathos. The victorious Greeks demand the liquidation of the whole house of Priam, and the only scion left, the infant Astyanax, is thrown from a tower and killed. His heart-broken grandmother Hecuba addresses the Greeks:

> O ye Argives, was your spear keen and your hearts so low and cold, to fear this babe? 'Twas a strange murder for brave men! For fear this babe some day might raise again his fallen land? Had ye so little pride? While Hector fought and thousands at his side, ye smote us and we perished; and now, now, when all are dead and Ilion lieth low ye dread this innocent![1]

And now turn to II Samuel ix. This is part of what is called the Court History of King David and is one of the earliest written sections of the Old Testament. Here is a similar case, a victorious commander seeking to know if there are left any of the family of his fallen enemy. And there is one.

> Now when Mephibosheth, the son of Jonathan, the son of Saul, was come unto David he fell on his face and did reverence. And David said Mephibosheth. And he answered, Behold thy servant. And David said unto him

[1] Gilbert Murray's translation.

Fear not: for I will surely show thee kindness for Jonathan thy father's sake and will restore thee all the land of Saul thy father: and thou shalt eat bread at my table continually.

And all this happened in Israel about six centuries before Euripides wrote his play.

A common theme of Greek tragedy was the sin of *hubris,* that over-weening pride in one's own achievements that must finally attract the anger of the gods. Æschylus' *Persae* is a variation on this theme. But so also is the story of Nebuchadnezzar in Daniel iv. The king is walking in the palace and says complacently, "Is not this great Babylon which I have built?"

While the word was in the king's mouth there fell a voice from heaven, saying "O King Nebuchadnezzar, to thee it is spoken: the Kingdom is departed from thee".

The Bible has its Utopias, but it is worth noticing of what quality they are. There is here no "Cockney paradise" as William Morris once scornfully described Edward Bellamy's *Looking Backward,* nor are we concerned with economic problems or problems of government. It is by seeking first the kingdom of God and His righteousness that everything else falls into line. Thus the Gospels. In Zechariah we have an earlier Utopia but of the same nature:

The streets of the city shall be full of boys and girls playing in the streets thereof . . . In that day there shall be upon the bells of the horses, HOLY UNTO THE LORD; and the pots in the Lord's house shall be like the bowls before the altar.

I have spoken of narrative. Let me add one more point to this. The Biblical writers have a fine appreciation of the value of climax. To the examples already given let me add two more from the narrative literature. The first is the well-known story of Belshazzar in Daniel v. A superb narrative tells of the feast which this king (unknown, by the way, to

E

history) gave to his lords, using the golden vessels stolen from the Temple at Jerusalem. When the excitement is at its height there appears some strange writing on the wall: "Then the king's countenance was changed in him and his thoughts troubled him". No one can interpret the writing save Daniel and he spells out the words of doom: "thou art weighed in the balances and art found wanting, thy kingdom is divided and given to the Medes and Persians". The king, poor man, honours Daniel for his skill in interpretation, but it is too late. "In that night was Belshazzar the king of the Chaldeans slain, and Darius the Mede took the kingdom."

The second is even more effective. It is from St. John's Gospel, chapter xiii.

> And when he had dipped the sop he gave it to Judas Iscariot, the son of Simon. And after the sop Satan entered into him. Then said Jesus unto him That thou doest, do quickly. . . . He then having received the sop went immediately out, and it was night.

6

We come now to a third correlation—that with history. On this there are certain considerations of method which I shall deal with in the next chapter. Here, however, we might notice one or two interesting facts.

A comparative table of dates is a useful thing to look at when studying history and nowhere more than when studying the Old Testament. In reading the Old Testament we feel that we are a long way ahead in the history by the time we come to Amos. We have had not only Abraham and the patriarchs but also Samuel, Saul, David and Solomon, and nearly two hundred years of the divided kingdom. Yet when Amos was thundering out an advanced social gospel to the complacent mid-Victorians of the court of Jeroboam II Rome was only in its beginnings and was represented by but a few mud huts on the banks of the Tiber. The Roman world in its thinking and its social life never caught up with Amos until the Republic and the Empire had run their course for a thousand years and the Empire had become Christian. And even then it is extremely doubtful whether by our own times we have fully appreciated his message. His date, however, was 753 B.C.

Then again we notice that Jerusalem fell to Babylon in 586 and the Exile began. This period is contemporary with the golden age of Athens but it precedes Buddha and Confucius by about a century. The battle of Marathon took place about the time of Malachi, while Plato is contemporary with Nehemiah's second visit to Jerusalem. Already, well before Pericles and Buddha, Israel had had a long history of foreign relations, and the empires of Syria, Assyria and Babylon had all passed away. Persia was soon to follow, and in the time of confusion that followed the death of Alexander the Great in 323 the Old Testament chronicler was writing the final native version of the history of Israel. These connections are so often forgotten or even unknown that the term "ancient history" is commonly used as applying only to the history of Greece and Rome with a little preliminary study of Egypt and Crete. If Western civilization is the product of three civilizations—Greece, Rome and Judæa—it is worth remembering that much the oldest and much the most universal contribution came from Judæa.

Ancient history, however, as written, whether Hebrew, Greek or any other, was not history in our sense of the word. It was written with a deliberate purpose of edification. Why, for example, does Thucydides in Book V give so much space to the discussion between Melos and Athens? Not because he was using a verbatim shorthand report. There was no such thing and the discussion was largely made up by Thucydides himself. But he wanted to show his contemporaries and posterity what a dreadful unforgivable crime this was, and how it preceded the disastrous Sicilian expedition in which Athens met the just vengeance of the gods.

Similarly the histories of Israel were written with a purpose. They express the prophetic judgements on events rather than an unbiased account of the events themselves. Accordingly they are written from the standpoint not of any sectional interest but of eternal right. This has been the attitude of prophets in every generation. They have had the knack of abstracting from contemporary events those elements that are of eternal significance and in the light of these have judged the events themselves. You get this in Mazzini, whose business it was to bring the working men of Italy in on the side of the revolution. His address to them in 1860 contains this remarkable passage:

> If you would withdraw yourselves from beneath the arbitrary rule and tyranny of men you must adore God.

There is something very much of the Hebrew prophet in this attitude.

Still more notable "prophetic" passages are to be found scattered throughout the works of Edmund Burke. Take, for instance, his speeches on American Taxation (April 18th, 1774) and on Conciliation with America (March 22nd, 1775) and you find this:

> I am not here going into the distinctions of right, nor attempting to mark their boundaries. I do not enter into those metaphysical distinctions.
>
> Magnanimity in politics is not seldom the truest wisdom, and a great empire and little minds go ill together.
>
> My hold on the colonies is in the close affection which grows from common names, from kindred blood, from similar privileges and equal protection. These are ties which though light as air are as strong as links of iron.

What could be more "prophetic" than that? Yet so little are the prophets heeded that it is doubtful whether in the whole length and breadth of the United States there is a single statue to Burke, although he understood, sympathized with and laboured to present the colonists' point of view more than any other Englishman of his time.

The New Testament also gains by a correlation with

history. Take, for instance, the famous second chapter of
the Epistle to the Philippians, which contains the "kenotic"
clause—"He emptied himself, taking the form of a servant".
What is the key phrase in this famous passage? Not "emptied"
—although that was the word that the Reformation theologians stressed. The context makes it clear that this is simply
one of a number of epithets all meaning the same thing. No.
The keyword is "Lord"—"the name which is above every
name". The background of this is the insane attitude of
Caligula, who made himself equal to Jupiter and wished to
have the Oriental title—Lord—κύριος—given to him by the
Senate. Julius Caesar and Augustus had started the cult of
emperor worship by acquiring the title "divus" but this was
not enough for Caligula and Nero. Now Philippi was a
garrison town and the soldiers were full of the gossip from
the capital. And to the small group of Christians who would
also be familiar with all the talk about this proposed new
title Paul writes:

> Christ Jesus, who being in the form of God counted it
> not a prize to be on an equality with God but emptied
> himself, taking the form of a servant—becoming obedient
> even unto death. . . .
> Wherefore also God hath highly exalted *him* [note
> where the emphasis comes] and gave unto *him* the name
> which is above every name, that at the name of *Jesus* every
> knee should bow . . . and that every tongue should confess
> that JESUS CHRIST is *LORD*, to the glory of God the
> Father.

And by the way, notice that climax. The word "Lord" is
kept to the very end and it would come as a thunderclap to
those who first heard it.

7

With all this, however, we must remember that the Bible
is a book of religion. It is not a book of science, although in
Genesis it goes into the origins of things. Nor is it a book of

history as we understand history. Its theme is God in nature and God in man and it speaks to all ages, all centuries, all nations, peoples and tongues, just because it speaks to man as man. Man at all times has loved and hated, worked and played, been frustrated and known success, has sinned and repented, experienced sorrow and joy. To this everlasting man who is to be found under all the veneers of rank and nationality and race, the Biblical writers address themselves. They knew that all the manifold activities of man are but phases of his one great activity—the discovery of the true law of his being. This is to be found only in God, but men have always been slow to recognize this and have usually died before finding it out. Hence the Bible is always contemporary. The Psalms speak to our own condition as they spoke to Cromwell's Ironsides or St. Bernard's monks. The words of Deuteronomy were always on the lips of Jesus and its humanity makes its appeal to ourselves. The unknown Chronicler puts into the mouth of Hezekiah, King of Judah, a great prayer which speaks to the condition of many of us:

> The good Lord pardon every one that setteth his heart to seek God, the Lord, the God of his fathers, though he be not cleansed according to the purification of the sanctuary.

And the parables of Jesus and the Epistles of Paul are also at one and the same moment contemporary and timeless.

Finally, like the Lord at the head of the Way in Bunyan's allegory who "had them up to the top of the gate and shewed them by what deed they were saved", an education in the Bible will bring home to every reader sooner or later that it is not just a story of how man finds God but also a record of what God has done for man. This may take a long while and more is needed than a mere reading of the text, but it is the text that tells us about it and interprets the conviction when it arrives.

CHAPTER IV

THE HISTORICAL METHOD

I

Is it not true that one of the most unfortunate technical terms ever invented is "Higher Criticism"? There is a flavour of superiority in the very words which not unnaturally added irritation to disagreement in its opponents. This irritation was increased when the term "Lower Criticism" had to be coined to indicate that which had hitherto been the only form of criticism recognized, namely, textual criticism. To characterize as "lower" (in *any* sense) the great work of Westcott and Hort seemed to be a quite gratuitous form of snobbery. And as if these were not enough the phrase "higher criticism" came to be made synonymous with the phrase "the modern use of the Bible", thus consigning to a limbo of antiquarianism all those scholars who lived before the elucidation of the various documents J. E. D. and P. The satirist might well write that our forefathers

> were content Mark, Matthew, Luke and John
> Should bless the old-fashioned Beds they lay upon:
> But we, for every one of theirs, have two,
> And trust the Watchfulness of blessed Q.[1]

And yet the thing itself is quite simple and quite inoffensive. For what it means is not "there are more than one Isaiahs" or "Job never lived" nor is the essence of it the sorting out of the various strands in the Pentateuchal narrative. It refers simply to a method of approach to the past which every historian has to use all the time and which every one of us, historian or not, uses some of the time whenever we

[1] R. A. Knox, *Absolute and Abitofhell.*

57

want to find out the truth of something concerning which we have no first-hand information.

For instance, I go away for a holiday and find that my favourite newspaper is unobtainable. I have to fall back on some other paper which I would never look at at home. Whatever it says about the present Government I take with a large grain of salt. I ask myself what is behind the printed word, who wrote it, why did he write it, who were his informants, were they reliable, and so I continue to itemize my curiosity. If we are students of history it is certainly useful to know whether a writer on the Reformation is a Catholic or a Protestant or primarily a scholar, just as in economics it is useful to know if the facts are being put before us by a Communist or a democrat.

2

Now are the narratives of the Bible in similar case? Certainly not, I can hear someone say. The Bible, after all, is somewhat different from *The Times* and the Tass agency. It is the word of God and it is the Book by which men have lived and died. It contains the documents of our faith.

Yet when we go into the matter it is not quite so simple as this. For one thing, there are extant no original manuscripts of any part of the Bible, not even of the New Testament, and those copies that we do possess show often considerable variations. Which, then, shall we say is the true word of God, the Codex Sinaiticus in the British Museum or the Codex Bezae at Cambridge? The marginal references of the English Revised Version show how difficult it is to decide. In a short book like Hosea, for example, there are hundreds of variant readings any one of which might represent the original text, but there is no means of discovering which it is.

But if we go in for the verbal inspiration of the Bible we must do it consistently. We cannot say that these differences are "merely verbal" and negligible and that we have the general sense to guide us. If it is the words that are the inspired message, then we must stick to the words. To depart from this practice is to become in some measure a "higher critic", which is simply to say that we use the same method that everybody has to use in assessing conflicting evidence. And the agreed text which we accept as a resultant of all these variants is a man-made thing, and if the inspiration is due to the Holy Spirit it can only be as it came through the scholars, Westcott and Hort, Liddell and Scott, Grimm and Thayer, Brown, Driver and Briggs and all the rest of them. Let there be no mistake about that. We cannot in these days recover any of the Biblical writings in their original form, not even the sayings of Jesus.

What, then, do we mean by calling the Bible the Word of God? It is a time-honoured term which expresses an obvious truth and so it cannot lightly be set aside. It cannot mean, however, that we have in it the Greek or Hebrew words spoken by God to the writers—although a great many people *do* think that is what it means. It can only properly mean that the Bible is the great book of religion. It exhibits the search of man for God, and as they have searched they have not only found Him but also been found *of* Him. The deepest experiences of their lives have wrought such conviction within them that it has been the very word of God Himself to their souls. The "Word" is not a literal word, a statement or a text, but a situation in which God Himself has been most surely believed to have taken part as an active initiating agent. The Bible both gives us the record of such experiences in the lives of men, expressed in the language forms and imagery of their own time, and also it has shown itself all down the ages to have the power to re-create similar experiences in the lives of other men. It is thus not just a record. It is a creative activity. To use the old phrase the Word of God is "lively" —both living and life-giving.

But literalism not only hinders the free running of the Word, it may actually warp it altogether. For example, somebody once expressed to Jesus the view that the good news of the kingdom is such that men will flock eagerly into it. But Jesus knew the human heart better than that, and he tells the man a story. The kingdom of Heaven is like a man who made a supper and sent to tell the guests that everything was now ready. But did they come? Not they. They all with one accord began to make excuses, or, as Matthew has it, "they made light of it and went their ways". So the host in a fury has to fill up their places with all the rag-tag and bob-tail of the neighbourhood. Such is the parable and the "moral" of it is obvious enough. But in the narrative there occurs this phrase, "go out into the highways and the hedges and compel them to come in". This remark, altogether isolated from its text, was used by St. Augustine to justify the use of force to compel people to be orthodox Christians. It was improved upon in later ages and the whole apparatus of torture was applied to Jews and heretics alike for the same end.

That the patience of God has its limits—a teaching flatly contradictory to that of Jesus—was justified by an isolated text which occurs in an old pagan myth embedded in Genesis vi, "my spirit shall not strive with man for ever"—made worse in this case because "strive" is a mistranslation of the Hebrew. A very doubtful addition to Matthew's Gospel—"Thou art Peter and upon this rock will I build my Church"—has been used to "prove" that the modern Papacy, the Vatican, College of Propaganda, Swiss guards and all, was authorized and indeed intended by Christ from the beginning. Race prejudice has been exalted into a Christian principle on the basis of Genesis ix. 25, which has been held to identify Ham the son of Canaan with the present Bantu people of Africa—false history, false anthropology and false exegesis, but look at the damage it has done! St. Paul's view that "the powers that be are ordained of God" has been used by Catholics and Protestants alike to justify almost any act of the State that played into the hands of the Church authorities or at any rate that did not conflict with them. Thus in wartime the Church has backed the State, and the Pope has blessed the banners both of Mussolini and of Franco, just as Luther had condoned the secular activities of the German princes.

And so we might go on. The point to notice is that once the principle is accepted that texts may properly be isolated from their contexts and that it is the words that matter, the tendency to self-justification is inherent in the principle itself. The warfare of texts which has disfigured Christian history has thus been inevitable and understandable. Nevertheless, it is well to note that noble spirits have always acted nobly even when applying a false theory, and even literalism has become for them a means of grace.

3

Our business, however, is with religious education, not with proselytism or propaganda, and fortunately the scholars of the last hundred years have made it possible. Once we give up misuse of texts and treat the Bible historically, which means taking its message as a whole and not as a patchwork of sayings, we open out before ourselves a most wonderful opportunity for study and devotion.

We step back into the situation of the people who heard the message for the first time and find out what it meant to *them*. We are concerned to know who the people were who wrote it and who the people were for whom it was written. We ask when it was written and why it was written and also how it was written. And if in the course of these enquiries we come across contradictions either of statements with one another—(how did the animals go into the ark; did they all go in two by two or were there two of one kind and seven of another?)—or of obvious fact—(how would all the animals get into the ark, anyway, and how could they be fed for all that length of time?)—or of moral standards—(what about the morality of Jacob compared with that of Jesus or even that of Amos?)—we shall not have to do violence either to our common sense or, what is more important, to the spiritual message of the Bible, by making our major task the safeguarding of the words as we find them.

How, for instance, is Judges v in any sense the word of
God? Here is the story of a treacherous woman who breaks
all the rules of hospitality and murders her guest while he is
asleep. For doing so she is lauded to the skies by the writer.
"Blessed above women shall Jael be . . . so let all thine enemies
perish O Lord." We can see for ourselves the horrible inconsistency of the Pope's thanksgiving to God for the massacre
of St. Bartholomew's Day; the magnificence of the language of
Judges v should not hide from us the equally horrible inconsistency of the writer. But that is not the end of the matter.
We have to ask who he was, when he wrote, what were the
moral standards of his time, why did he write and finally why
was the passage retained in a book which includes Isaiah liii
and the Gospels.

These are vital questions but they are all capable of
scholarly answers which make for understanding of the
situation. There are various ways of avoiding an answer. I
have indicated one of them—namely to take the text as it
stands and shake one's head at the mysterious ways of Providence in "inspiring" such writings. I must now mention
another which in some quarters is becoming popular today.

It has been realized that once you accept the historical
method you must accept it throughout. This applies equally to
the documents of the American Revolution, to the various
lives of Francis of Assisi, to the Bible and to Church history
and the creeds. It is known, however, that on certain
denominational positions this method has a very solvent
effect. The verdict of history is not always given in one's own
favour. Some men, even, to some extent, the late Bishop
Gore, therefore drew distinctions. They allowed the historical method in full with regard to the Old Testament, less
so to the New Testament and not at all to the early history of
the Church and the Councils. The inconsistency and indeed
the impossibility of this position is clear and so the method
itself has been abandoned by certain recent writers. For the
interpretation of the Old Testament they fall back not on
fundamentalism of the old kind but on allegory. They are

thereby still able to hold that the majority decisions of the Councils of Nicaea and Chalcedon were inspired by God while they get rid of the difficulties of the inspiration of the Old Testament by declaring the whole thing to be an allegory of the *Christian* faith. The foundation of this position is not in scholarship at all but in denominationalism. It is an old form of theological escapism and in the Middle Ages it had the great advantage of allowing a man to make the Bible mean what he himself wanted it to mean while still remaining "orthodox".

On the Protestant side the inconveniences of the historical method have been felt in a different way. The so-called neo-Calvinist group have taken up with regard to the Bible a position similar to that of the Anglo-Catholics with regard to the Church. Indeed, we are witnessing in our time a revival of the rival orthodoxies of the sixteenth century, not, however, as great historical movements of the spirit carrying with them a revival of religion but rather as competitive academic ideologies. As evangelical Protestantism is considered by the Anglo-Catholic school to be the enemy, so liberalism is looked on by the neo-Calvinists as the enemy.

But liberalism of the type of Glover's *Jesus of History* sprang out of the historical method. It showed us Jesus not only as a real man—which the Church has always believed or tried to believe—but also as a man contemporary with His own age, and often no more than that. This, of course, took away from the Bible any particularly supernatural reference and is seen in its most extreme form in Bishop Barnes' book *The Origins of Christianity*. The historical method itself therefore became suspect, and in order to find a presumably sure basis for supernaturalism the Bible had again to be taken as it stood—not, however, in isolated texts after the manner of the older fundamentalists but in whole books, passages and situations—allowing for variations in this or that statement, but always assuming that the situation as a whole was as recorded. Particularly was this the case with St. Paul's Epistles. The historical background was ignored, the *ad hoc* nature of the writing themselves was discounted, and they

were taken as expositions of a definite doctrine called
"Paulinism".

4

It is time, therefore, to come to the historical method
itself. Essentially it consists in placing the narrative back in
the setting within which it originated. This setting includes
both the historical background and also the character and
purpose of the writer. To find these out it is necessary to
consider the form in which the narrative has come down to us
—how near it is to the events with which it deals, how uni-
form it is, and what was the date at which it was written.
These preliminaries are not themselves the historical method,
although they are often considered to be so. The historical
view of the Bible does not come into sight until these have
been dealt with. We begin, therefore, with the fact that the
Bible contains the history of a people from about the year
1500 B.C. to about the year A.D. 100. The earliest parts of the
Old Testament are the ballads telling of battles long ago, such
as the song of Deborah in Judges v, and fables and proverbs
handed down by word of mouth from untold generations,
such as the fable of the trees that elected a king (Judges ix),
and the riddles proposed by Samson to the Philistines. These
were incorporated into the history when it came to be
written, and indeed a good deal of early history is written
round older stories and place names to give a colour of history
to that which is strictly traditional.

You will have noticed, for instance, how clever it was of
Gideon to slaughter the prince Oreb at the rock Oreb, and
to catch up with Zeeb at the very winepress that bore his
name (Judges vii. 25)! In these cases the story probably
follows the name, rather than the reverse. Often the later
chronicler, mindful of the tradition that had endured to his
day, credited his ancestors with the foresight that it would be
so. "When your children shall ask their fathers in time to
come, saying, What mean these stones? then ye shall let your
children know, saying, Israel came over this Jordan on dry

land—wherefore the name of that place was called Gilgal unto this day."[1] This was written long after the event but was antedated in this way.

The earliest histories of the nation would probably be sung rather than written. Then when the kingdom divided after the days of Solomon, both the North and the South became greatly concerned with their ancestry and so they wrote down their history each with a pardonable bias toward its own point of view. When the two accounts came to be combined after the dissolution of the northern kingdom no attempt was made to smooth out the contradictions between the two accounts, and hence the bewilderment of the modern reader who finds that "the Bible contradicts itself".

This brings us to a characteristic of ancient writings which the historical method of study must recognize. The ancients had no idea of "collation". If a modern writer finds two differing accounts of the same event he tries to "collate" them and arrive at a coherent narrative, and so out of materials themselves only partly true he tries to construct the truth. This means considering the reasons for the difference of the texts, the bias of each authority, the time and the purpose of the writing, and all those other considerations which come under the heading of what the scholars call "diplomatic". The ancient writers cared nothing about this. Whatever was not flatly contradictory to their own point of view went in just as it was, and the differences did not worry either the writer or his reader. Nowadays, however, the reader must do for himself what the ancients did not do for him. He must try to get the truth of the matter or, if that cannot be done, to find out at any rate all he can to account for the differences.

A second characteristic of ancient writers was their persistent ignoring of what we call secondary causes. We keep up the same habit among ourselves when we say, for instance,

---

[1] Joshua iv. 21-v. 9. The name Gilgal means "rolling", a curious name for a place. But the writer hits upon an explanation, "the Lord said to Joshua, This day have I *rolled away* the reproach of Egypt from off you".

"Ranulf Flambard built Durham Cathedral". Flambard was justiciar of the realm of England and not a builder at all. But he employed an architect, who again was not himself a builder. The architect employed workmen who did the actual building. Flambard, however, was the first cause, the others were secondary; and—following a common practice—we go back to the originator of the idea and credit him with the whole work. The ancient writer went back always to the first cause, and to him the first cause was always God.

Pharaoh's heart is hard and he will not let the children of Israel go. Why? There can only be one answer to this if you go back far enough. God must have hardened his heart. Pharaoh was drowned in the Red Sea. Why? God must have done that too. And the fact that he was drowned by God because his heart was hard and that God had hardened his heart, looks to us like an ethical confusion, but to the ancients it was no confusion at all. It was a normal way of accounting for things otherwise inexplicable. It was even used to explain the extraordinary fact that despite the word of God plainly declared by the prophets the people did not listen (Isaiah vi. 9, 10), and in the New Testament this was held to be the only reason why the Jews rejected the Messiah (Matthew xiii. 14, 15, etc.). God had determined it to be so. In the Middle Ages they accounted for plague in the same way. It was due not to drains or infection or rats. It was due simply to God.

In the Bible, however, this cavalier habit of saddling the Almighty with everything produces a very real difficulty, for it was not only external events that were put down to God. He was also responsible for a man's state of mind. Consequently when Amos is disgusted with the luxury and vice of the court of Jeroboam II and is convinced that the end will be disaster, he says not, "I tell you for certain that this will bring decay and defeat to Israel" but, "Thus saith the Lord. I will press you, and flight shall perish from the swift, neither shall the mighty deliver himself". It is all put into the mouth of God, and to the modern reader it sounds as if God had literally said these words into the ear of the prophet. That, of course, is precisely what the prophet himself believed. Whence could come such ideas if not from God?

We keep the same idea among ourselves in the second collect at evening prayer which begins, "O God, from whom all holy desires, all good counsels, and all just works do proceed". It looks at first sight as if it deprived men of all responsibility for their own thoughts and actions. In reality it is a Hebrew- or rather a primitive-idiom, for all primitive peoples think in this way. What a man says under stress of conviction or the inspiration of insight is therefore still his own idea, and it does not have to be removed from critical consideration just because he attributes it to God. Isaiah's conviction—"Thus saith the Lord"—was that "Zion shall be redeemed" (i. 27) and "thine eyes shall see Jerusalem a quiet habitation, a tent that shall not be removed—for the Lord is our king; he will save us" (xxxiii. 20, 22). Micah, the working man who was a bit more realistic than his aristocratic contemporary, also said, "Thus saith the Lord", but in his case it was that "Zion shall be plowed as a field and Jerusalem shall become heaps". And it was Micah's conviction and not Isaiah's that was justified by the events.

A third characteristic of ancient writing which the modern reader must remember is that there was no law of copyright. Any writing was free to anybody to take and to use as he liked. If a man's work bore a certain resemblance to something already written and known and appreciated, his writings would be attached to the earlier book and be known under the same name. Thus "Isaiah" is the name not only of a man but also of a book, and the book contains material written in the days of Hezekiah before the exile to Babylon and other material written in the days of Cyrus when the exile was about to end, but the one name covers both. Yet even the English reader cannot fail to notice the differences in date, for the names of the kings are given. Again, Solomon had a reputation for wisdom, or rather (for he was anything but a wise man) for wise sayings. So a collector of proverbs, some of which are stated in so many words to be proverbs of Agur and others of Lemuel, put them all in together as the wise sayings of Solomon. Solomon's name had good publicity value and was used in precisely the same way as we ourselves get famous people to write prefaces to books by people not famous at all, so that the name that is known carries the work by the person whose name is unknown. It is no more dishonest in the one case than it is in the other. It was, at any rate, a well-established practice in ancient Israel, and Moses, Samuel, David, Isaiah and many more were all made use of in this way.

5

We are now able to lay down a certain order of procedure in dealing with any difficulties that arise in Bible study. Our canon would be this: Deal with the literary question first. It may be found that this is all that is necessary. If, however, it is not enough we then consider the historical situation. Not till this has been fully explored do we tackle the moral or ethical problem, if indeed it still remains.

Let us take an example. We are told that Jesus once cured a lunatic who had a legion of devils, and that He sent the unemployed devils into a herd of swine. "And the herd rushed down the steep into the sea, in number about two thousand." (Mark v. 1-20.)

That, on the face of it, was an immoral thing to do. The wretched owners saw their whole livelihood gone, apparently by an arbitrary act of Jesus. Commentators of an earlier day wrestled with this problem. They did not care to accuse Jesus of injustice, but neither did they want to throw doubts on the accuracy of the narrative as it stands. So it was said that these people were Jews, that Jews ought not to keep pigs and that Jesus punished them for so doing—arguments every one of which is completely gratuitous. We cannot imagine that Jesus could ever treat people in this way, and if the text says He did we may be sure that something has gone wrong with the text. This comes of treating the incident as a moral problem which presupposes taking the text as it is.

But if we assume at once that our Lord would never do anything so alien to His character as this, we may then proceed by starting with the literary question. Is the story reported as it happened? The answer surely is that *both* incidents undoubtedly happened—the lunatic was cured and the pigs did stampede. But the connection between them is in the mind of the writer—it is his way of linking up two extraordinary events which happened about the same time, and *therefore,* he would argue, as indeed every ancient writer would argue, must be connected. Thus there is no moral problem to be argued at all. All that is at stake is a literary convention of the first century A.D.

The story of Jonah is an obvious example in the Old Testament. Was Jonah swallowed by a whale? Can whales in any case swallow anything bigger than plankton? The most incredible *tours de force* have been executed in order to justify the narrative as it stands. The natural history of whales has been re-written with all the technicalities of pseudo-science in order to show that some very special kind of whale unknown to zoologists in some very special situation unknown to anybody might, and therefore once did, swallow a man. Moreover, it has been held to be possible that man can exist for three days inside a fish without suffocating. Alternatively, whales do not naturally swallow men and men do not naturally continue to live without air, and so the event was a miracle and there is nothing more to be done about it. You just have to accept it or, say some, you are not a Christian! The clinching "proof" of this is that Jesus and His contemporaries apparently looked on the story as historical. This may be so, although Matthew xii. 40 shows that the reference to the whale is treated as an allegory and the real point of the Jonah story—the repentance of the men of Nineveh—is brought out in the verse following.

The story of Jonah is a moral lesson cast, after the manner of the Biblical writers, in the form of a story. It is a protest against the violent racialism that disfigured Jewish life after the exile. Jonah, like the Jews, is unconcerned about the heathen, he wants them to perish and he will not lift a finger to save them. But when he himself falls into the hands of the heathen and they are all in deadly peril, the despised heathen do all in their power to save *him* (i. 13). So finally he has to go and preach to the heathen in a place called, for purposes of the story, Nineveh, and to Jonah's annoyance the heathen repent and God spares them. The story is concerned not so much with the redemption of the heathen, as with the redemption of Jonah. Once the historical setting of this story is appreciated the need to apologize for the whale vanishes away.

6

It would not be strictly true to say that the historical parts of the Old Testament were written by the prophets, yet that is almost the case. All history writing is a matter of selection and the reader has to allow for the principle on which the selection is made. Take the case of Omri. To the Assyrians, as we see from their inscriptions, the name of Omri, King of Israel, was one to be conjured with. He gave Israel a strategic new capital, he made alliances with neighbouring rulers, and he left a name which was attached to his country for years afterwards. Even Jehu, the scoundrel who wiped out the house of Omri altogether, is referred to on the inscriptions as the "son of Omri". But all that the Bible has to say about him is contained in four verses of I Kings xvi, and they are none of them complimentary. For like Jeroboam the son of Nebat he, too, "made Israel to sin". Clearly there is here at work some principle of selection which was not the same as that recognized by the Assyrians, or indeed by anybody except people to whom the pure worship and service of God was the primary concern. And that, of course, was the point of view of the Hebrew prophets.

The history of the Old Testament as we now have it contains, as we have seen, much early material. The codes of law, for example, were among the earliest sources. But all these early sources were worked over again and again chiefly by men who shared what is called the Deuteronomic point of view—a point of view not confined to the book of Deuteronomy but characteristic of all the eighth-century prophets and their successors. They had a concern not only for the holiness of God but also for humanity. Amos denounces the King of Edom because "he did cast off all pity and his anger did tear perpetually" (i. 11) but he equally denounces Moab for its inhumanity to Edom (ii. 1). The history, therefore, as it has come down to us is not history in our sense of the word —it is edification; and those events which make for edification are emphasized and those which do not are hurried over or omitted. The Hebrew Bible itself indicates this policy by its very arrangement. Joshua, Judges, Samuel and Kings are called not "histories", as we might think, but "the Former Prophets", while Isaiah, Jeremiah, Ezekiel and the "minor" prophets are "the Latter Prophets". The Hebrews clearly conceived of history as a branch of prophecy.

This connection of history and prophecy is the clue to the prophetic attitude. The prophets were concerned with events, and every single book of prophecy has a contemporary situation in mind. It is most important to realize this date-and-fact reference in everything the prophets said and wrote. They were not writing for the twentieth century A.D.—they were writing for their own day and generation.

Their attitude, however, to events was altogether peculiar. They never saw them as *simply* contemporary. They believed that with the contingency of every event there was also a constant element which raised it from being a mere casual happening into something which had eternal significance. But in view of the fashion already mentioned (pp. 62 f.) of treating the Old Testament simply as allegory, it is important to realize that to the prophets the eternal significance was, so to speak, part and parcel of the event itself. It could not exist at all without the actual date and fact, it was not a truth of which the event was simply an illustration, and, once grasped, the event itself became unimportant. *Both* factors were present, and each was necessary to the other. There is an incarnational view of truth even in the Old Testament. It was this which enabled Isaiah to give Hezekiah guidance as to his foreign policy with the assurance that "thus saith the Lord". Jeremiah was keenly aware of this divine urge in events even when he himself profoundly wished the events to be otherwise than what they were. And the cardinal event of all, the deliverance of Israel from Egypt, an event datable between 1400 and 1100 B.C., was quite inexplicable save as a manifestation of the power of God.

When they came to write about these things they introduced God as an interlocutor in the events themselves. It is God, for instance, who personally talks with Moses on Mount Sinai as one person might talk with another, but if we explain this as simply a primitive belief we miss the whole point of prophecy. Whether God actually talked to men or not, whether he was known to them as fire, earthquake, wind or a still small voice, the event itself manifested his presence. "Tell of all his mighty acts," says a psalmist, "sing of all his excellent greatness." It is this which distinguishes the Bible from all the other books of religion. Men approached God—or, to put it the other way round, God reveals Himself to men—in things that actually happen.

In teaching the Bible, therefore, it is important to remember that all its history and all its prophecy is there because it is all about God. It may be about Abraham, or David or Micah, but it is also about God. And this attitude to events is carried by the psalmists into the most personal and intimate life of the individual. When one of them with profound insight declares of God "against thee only have I sinned" he sums up in one pregnant sentence the whole prophetic view of life and destiny. It is the correlative of the conviction "Thou art my God". Accordingly our question is not, "What does this story teach us?"—whether it is the story of Joseph or Samuel or Mephibosheth or Naboth. The question to ask is, "What is this story *in itself*?" What does the writer understand by it? At what point do we see God in the story? Only then shall we understand the integral relationship of the constant and the contingent in the Biblical view of history.

It is a curious thing that this conviction, so fundamental in Hebrew religion, is today being hailed as the great discovery of Kierkegaard, the nineteenth-century Danish thinker. According to him a man only begins to "exist" when the eternal becomes for him an active principle in the temporal and he wholeheartedly commits himself to it. But this has always been recognized by all honest men as the very stuff of life. It is expressed in immortal verse by Shelley in the great lines at the close of *Prometheus Unbound*. But in Hebrew religion this commitment is not to an idea or to a cause but to God, the God who had slowly revealed Himself in history.

7

It is pretty well an accepted fact that the New Testament is a more difficult subject of religious education than the Old. One reason is that there is less of it. The Gospels are very short, and yet the life of Christ is a theme which must enter in some form into every stage of the teaching. If the Acts of the Apostles is attempted it is soon exhausted, and less imaginative teachers content themselves with seeing that the children can trace the routes of St. Paul's missionary journeys—as if it mattered. The Epistles are uniformly held to be "very difficult", although we do well to realize that they were sent in the first place to people who had much less education than a boy or girl at our School Certificate stage. The book of Revelation is left on one side as a playground for British Israelites, Christadelphians and other groups of the theological underworld.

Over against this the Old Testament is full of colour and variety. There is a thousand years of development, a panoramic view of one ancient empire after another occupying the stage of history, there is poetry, speculation, history, politics, myth, legend, oratory, and every conceivable kind of personal and public interest, all of it centred round a growing revelation of God to His people. There is something there for all ages and all stages of experience.

Then again the New Testament seems to be clouded over with doctrine. We have to face such questions as the nature of Christ—naturally nobody ever asks about the nature of Jeremiah—the Virgin Birth, the Trinity, the meaning of Christ's death, the miracles, heaven and hell. If we take up the Epistles we find a whole catalogue of experiences which the believer is expected to undergo—redemption, justification, sanctification, election, and a few more, none of which is as much as mentioned in any standard book on psychology. Such questions as these may possibly arise in the Old Testament, but the "historical method" seems to provide against the necessity of taking them too seriously. To see these things "in their setting" is to see them as they are, but the setting of the New Testament seems to be as much twentieth century as first, and the historical method offers no consolations.

At the root of these problems is another more fundamental. What exactly is the religion into which we are seeking to educate our people? Is it the religion that Jesus Himself had and is supposed to exemplify, or is it the religion in which Jesus Himself is the centre of worship and which was elaborated by St. Paul?

This alternative does not appear at all stages. Clearly with younger children the religion of Jesus Himself is the most natural to emphasize. Jesus' own attitude to God, to other people, to animals, to sickness and disease is the chief concern of the teacher in the earlier stages. This was the religion which that greatest of all teachers of young children, Froebel, professed, and for his purpose he felt it to be adequate. It is not at this stage that the alternative offers itself.

But it most certainly appears later. The New England school of writers and poets—Whittier, Emerson, Longfellow, Oliver Wendell Holmes and others—were all of them apostles of the religion of Jesus Himself. To follow in His steps was the duty of every sensible person, and all it seemed to need was willingness to start. This attitude, if not entirely "moon-struck with optimism" as William James said of Emerson, was at any rate singularly blind to the sinfulness of sin. The chief function of Christianity was amelioration, and there was about it a certain "inevitability of gradualness". Whittier perhaps saw beyond this—

> Thou judgest us, Thy purity
> Doth all our lusts condemn.
> The love that draws us nearer thee
> Is hot with wrath to them—

but his attitude to it was largely inarticulate. Compare almost any of Whittier's hymns with the hymns of Charles Wesley or Isaac Watts, and the difference is obvious at once. To one school of thought Jesus is the perfect pattern, the leader, the brother and friend, whose character is a standing reproach to us. To the other He is the word of God in our universe, our Saviour and Lord, who "demands my soul, my life, my all". This last was what Jesus was to Paul and that is why the Christ of faith appears so different from the Jesus of history.

Then the very reasonableness of the historical method applied to the Old Testament creates a difficulty in the study of the New. We have so completely recovered the background of the first century that we are apt to see in Christ no more than a culmination of contemporary tendencies. Moreover, the historical method, when applied to the New Testament, creates difficulties of its own. Bishop Gore, as we have seen, altogether refused to apply it to the period of the great Creeds. Yet history of whatever period or subject is still history and the same canons of interpretation apply throughout. If consideration of thought forms of ancient writers explains away the story of Elisha and the axe (II Kings vi. 4-7)—and we have to remember that the Old Testament itself shows us how legends arise (see II Kings iii. 20-23)—does it not also explain away the story of the feeding of the five thousand and indeed of the Resurrection itself? The reasonableness of the treatment of the Resurrection story as by the author of *By an*

Unknown Disciple hides from us the radical nature of the method employed.   And when we come to Nicaea with its party politics, its lobbying, its manipulation of votes, might not the conclusion be drawn that far from being a demonstration of the Holy Spirit we have here a political party Convention under another name?

All such questions, whether reasonable or not, affect not only history but also *faith*, and increase the difficulty of teaching the New Testament with conviction. The excesses of recent Form-Criticism have still further appeared to shake the assurance of people in the certainty that here in the Gospels we have the very words of Christ. It is curious, however, that the one book in the New Testament to which the historical method could be most easily applied without any qualms— —Revelation—is the book usually omitted from consideration altogether.

8

What, then, are the standards which we must bring to the study of the New Testament to be intellectually honest and yet not to lose the spiritual values which it has had for men at all times?

We have to accept the plain fact that nowhere in the New Testament can we be certain that we have the actual words spoken by our Lord. This is true even of the Greek text, for even if it were a verbatim translation, it nevertheless is a translation, for our Lord spoke in Aramaic. The only places where we are likely to have the words He Himself used are those where the Aramaic original is given—e.g. *Talitha Cumi, Ephphatha*, and the cry of dereliction, *Eloi, eloi, lama sabachthani*. To many people this is a difficulty which they cannot overcome, and yet it has been known from very early times.   The so-called "High-priestly prayer" of Jesus in John xvii is quite clearly not a verbatim account written on the spot by a reporter, nor are the accounts of the Temptation in Matthew and Luke.

Yet despite this obvious truth and despite the negative

results of Schweitzer's *Quest of the Historical Jesus* and of the Eschatological and Form-criticism schools, an agnostic conclusion is quite unwarranted. It is not true that we cannot find the historical Jesus. There is no need whatever either to sacrifice history for "the Christ of experience", or, like Roman Catholics and Fundamentalists, to reaffirm dogmatically a self-styled "orthodoxy" and in the face of all modern scholarship to uphold such positions as the primacy of Matthew's Gospel and the Pauline authorship of Hebrews. The most remarkable feature of the Synoptic Gospels is not their differences but their agreement. The picture that they give of Jesus is an astonishingly coherent one and the cumulative effect of the three accounts has always carried conviction.

The differences themselves are a guarantee of genuineness, for had the accounts been manufactured out of a myth there would certainly have been some attempt at uniformity among the details. We have to rely not on this or that text, the literal accuracy of which no man can guarantee, but rather on the effect of the story as a whole, and in that case there is no doubt whatever. Even the differences in the Resurrection story as to whether there was one angel at the tomb (Matthew), or two men (Luke), or a young man (Mark), or two angels (John), indicate that something so tremendous had happened that the actual details of it were lost on confused recollection.

The standard, therefore, must always be not the inerrancy of the text (which is unobtainable) but the character of Jesus as revealed in the Gospels. Is such and such a text or is such and such an act in conformity with the character of Jesus? We have already appealed to this standard in the story of the Gadarene lunatic and it should be clear that it is perfectly applicable. We may also apply it to the many misinterpretations of the references to Peter's power of "binding and loosing" and ask ourselves if they are consonant with Jesus' character or are they upheld on totally other grounds? Paul himself takes this line and draws a distinction between what is of himself and what is "of the Lord", and the things that are "of the Lord" are never isolated quotations of words but a reference to Jesus, who is a person of known character.

Nor need we be slavish even about our canon of interpretation any more than we should be slavish about the text. A book which had a great vogue at the beginning of the century was C. M. Sheldon's *In His Steps, or What Would Jesus Do?* in which it was attempted to form a code of conduct out of the words of the Gospels. This was but another form of literalism and with some people it had the oddly negative result of forbidding all the things that Jesus did *not* do!

With our standard in mind we can turn to the New Testament and recognize that we are still concerned as in the Old Testament with an ancient people with ancient forms of thought. They put two and two together in their own way. They had no sense of copyright or of the need for collation. They had no real grasp of secondary causes and unless an event was so plain as to be unmistakable they at once put it down to a special providence. Tertullian complains that this is so with the heathen of his own day who ignore the obvious natural causes of the rising and falling of the Tiber or the Nile and blame them upon some special magical dirty work of the Christians.[1]

The New Testament writers saw things in pictorial form and had little abstract terminology. Even the "long words" used by Paul such as "justification" and the like are not abstract terms at all but are live metaphors borrowed from the law courts or other institutions that were flourishing at his time. It is completely misleading to think of Old Testament writers as primitive people writing in primitive ways, and then to think of Paul and the others as compiling a theological treatise for submission as it stands to scholars of the twentieth century.

9

In the New Testament we are still within the orbit of Jewish thought. It would appear that in the providence of

[1] *Apology*, c. 40.

God the destruction of Jerusalem in A.D. 70 was necessary in order that the Gospel might be saved from continuing as a sect of Judaism, but this is to attribute to circumstances something which was much more deliberate. It was Paul and not the son of Vespasian who thus liberated the Gospel, and he did it not by cutting Christianity off from its Jewish roots but by following his master's declaration that he was come not to destroy but to fulfil. For contemporary Rabbinism Paul certainly showed little use, although he understood its methods well enough and used them as an *argumentum ad hominem* when the case required it,[1] but for the Old Testament he had the utmost veneration. Jesus Himself went back to Isaiah and Deuteronomy and the Psalms and from these came again to His own times along a line quite different from that followed by post-exilic Judaism. In the same way Paul went back to the prophetic doctrine of the chosen people and returned with the doctrine that the Christian Church was the continuing Israel of God, thus by-passing the post-exilic doctrine which narrowed the conception down to that of an exclusive self-absorbed clique.

We are thus still in the realm of Jewish ideas, although they are the ideas of the sixth century B.C., taken up, revived and made fruitful, rather than the ideas of the Judaism of the first century A.D. It is only later that Christian theology takes a new turn in a world alien from that of its origins. Meanwhile the character of Jesus is clearly the standard by which the Old Testament is to be judged. Some parts of it pass away—"Ye have heard that it was said by them of old time . . . but I say unto you . . ." But its essential prophetic message does not pass away. The interpretation of Isaiah liii in the light of the life and death of Christ is more than a tribute to the insight of the early Church. It is also a vindication of the value of the Old Testament *in its own right* during all the six centuries before the death of Christ. God had indeed spoken to the fathers in the prophets, and the ideal Israelite whom they had in mind but

[1] e.g. in Galatians iv. and I Corinthians x. 4.

whom they had never fully seen was just such as Christ turned
out to be.

Consequently it is the inward life, the inward covenant of
Jeremiah, the self-interpreting and renewing word of God,
that is revealed both in this long history and in the new
revelation in Christ. So firmly rooted is this belief in the
minds of the first Christians that they later admitted into the
very text of the Gospels a story which most admirably
illustrates the mind of Christ, although the story itself was
apparently not known to the author of the Fourth Gospel into
which it was inserted. This is the well-known story of the
woman taken in adultery as found in John vii. 53 to viii. 11.
It is in the light of that characteristic story and not in the light
of later Christian rigorism that both the report of Jesus'
teaching about divorce in Matthew xix has to be judged and
also guidance for ourselves is to be discovered. No principle
is laid down, no code, no infallible rule. The appeal is always
to the total good of the persons concerned as it emerges in the
situation in which they are found at the moment. In other
words it is an appeal to an inward witness and not to an
outward law. Spiritual things are discerned spiritually.

10

It is here where the Fourth Gospel creates a very difficult
problem. It seems to go flatly against the witness of the
Synoptists. Jesus makes enormous claims for Himself. There
is an atmosphere of argumentation and at times almost of
querulousness, and Jesus' notable actions are enhanced not
even as miracles as in the Synoptics, where Jesus constantly
deprecates them, but as "signs" deliberately done in order
to convince people that He was the son of God. Too much, of
course, can easily be made of these differences. There are
warm human touches in the Fourth Gospel and there are
"Johannine" touches in the Synoptics (Matthew xi. 27). But
the Fourth Gospel is so unique in its point of view and so
intellectual in its standard of truth as compared with the

Synoptics, and even with the Epistles, that it clearly belongs to a different type of literature altogether and has to be interpreted as such.   On the surface it is possible to have sympathy with the ruthlessly frank schoolboy who said he didn't like St. John's Gospel because "Jesus was so conceited", but it is precisely here where we have to apply the canons of interpretation laid down earlier (page 68).

The first question to clear up is the literary one, and it will be found that with this most other difficulties disappear. The Fourth Gospel is a work of edification and not of biography, but it follows the conventions of Graeco-Roman authors from Plato and Thucydides onwards.   Truth is embodied not in a tale but in a dialogue and in a speech. The words put into the mouth of Jesus are the author's words and represent summaries of his own belief about our Lord. They are well founded but if the Synoptic portrait is the correct one none of these long speeches can be taken as the actual words of Jesus. The Lord who taught people in parables and was so tender towards the simple and the stupid is very unlike the person who scores verbal victories over the woman at the well.   Yet the view of Jesus—not His character but His position with His followers—given to us in that story is vital for the understanding of the Gospel as a whole. The charge of being "conceited" disappears when these literary conventions are made clear. Similarly the endless and at times, if we take them literally, unedifying wrangles with the Jews become luminous and significant if we see in them the author's attempt in his own style, as Paul had earlier attempted in his, to show just where the line was to be drawn between Christianity and Judaism. What is really strange in the Fourth Gospel is to find no reference to the Last Supper, but instead the insertion of a story more characteristic of the Synoptic Gospels, namely that of Jesus washing the disciples' feet, with its plain admonition, "If I, your Lord and master, have washed your feet ye also ought to wash one another's feet".

That the life of Christ was regulative for the Christian

community accounts for the ultimate appearance of Mark's Gospel long after the Pauline churches had been founded and the Epistles had been written. *Acts* continually refers to the disciples as followers of "the Way". It was expounded to new converts by Paul and they were introduced into a new community pledged to follow the Way. But it was not until the Gospels either as we have them or in an earlier form were produced that "the Way" was made clear for all to see. They naturally give only selections from the life of Christ but these selections are made to illustrate "the Way". We have already seen how important is the Jesus of history for the life of faith. Far from the founding of the Churches making the writing of the life of Christ unnecessary, some written account was clearly needed to provide a standard in any case for those who did not have the Jewish Scriptures, but also, and perhaps even more, for those who had them.

CHAPTER V

STAGES OF GROWTH

I

BUT the relevance of the historical method is not to the written word only; it concerns also the reader. He also grows and develops. If the idea of God gradually becomes purified, or, to put it the other way round, if God shows Himself to men "with revelation suited to their growth", the teacher has to remember that what history is to the community, experience is to the individual, and what Henry Scougal called "the life of God in the soul of man" has also its laws of development.

When there was a general belief in verbal inspiration a child was supposed to get equal spiritual sustenance from any part of the Bible, for texts of the Bible itself taken from anywhere were supposed to have the magic property of transforming words into character. But in the last two or three generations we have learned a great deal, not only about the Bible but also about the psychology of children, adolescents and adults. It is now nearly fifty years ago since the first serious attempt was made to grade Sunday school work according to the capacity of the child, intellectual and spiritual. Men of insight had long recognized the laws of spiritual change and growth, so that it was really an application of old knowledge rather than discovery. The idea is both implicit and explicit in the poetry of Wordsworth, and Froebel put it in epigrammatic form in the great saying: "the child has the right to be at each stage what that stage requires".

What then, in the case of children, are the stages of growth to which the adaptation of Bible teaching must conform?

The age of puberty is clearly one natural stage and after that the age of adolescence is a well-marked period with an obviously earlier period to about seventeen in the case of boys and rather younger in the case of girls, and a later period to about twenty-two. The stages before puberty are more difficult to determine, but there are probably four—say, infancy to about five; from five to seven or eight; from eight to eleven; and from eleven to the age of puberty. The most difficult period of development is that of puberty and early adolescence, for it is much the most primitive. It is more primitive than early childhood when the child more or less naturally conforms to the type of life which he finds around him, and it is more primitive than later adolescence. Adolescence itself is a kind of purgatorial period scarcely found at all in a primitive society, but becoming more and more extended with the development of civilization. The primitive child steps at initiation straight into adult responsibility—at puberty he becomes a member of the tribe. Adolescence is really a creation of society and the *sturm und drang* which is the romantic characteristic of the later stages of this period is due to rebellion against the conventions of a society which the adolescent is expected at once to accept, although as a matter of fact he scarcely ever does. Yet adults go on hoping for the best, for there is a certain amnesia about human development which causes the lessons learned in youth to become forgotten in the adult state, and age finds it extremely difficult to step back into its old skin.

2

We may thus take these six grades—infancy, childhood from five to eight, and eight to eleven, puberty, early adolescence and later adolescence—as a basis of the grading of our teaching material. Are there any special characteristics of each period which differentiate it from the others more than merely its place in the sequence?

(i) *Infancy*. It did not need Freud to tell us how important are these early years. It is during these that the foundation pattern of life is laid down, and everything depends on the small community within which the child grows up. The child, like the primitive, recognizes no clear line between "natural" and "supernatural", so that God can be almost as natural to him as his father and mother. He is also very sensitive to atmosphere, and differences between father and mother and any latent unhappiness register themselves on his mind as surely as do love and kindliness. Accordingly, religious ideas and the pattern of behaviour are unconsciously accepted by him through suggestion, and a sense of worship is easily awakened.

In nursery schools and departments, therefore, religious education consists in strengthening in the child the sense of security and confidence which in older people is the highest product of faith. The fatherhood and the love of God will scarcely be realizable by a child who has not known much earthly affection. Where the right personal relationships are present worship comes easily, for it is the formal (and small children appreciate formality) expression of thankfulness and happiness. The "morning ring" in the nursery school round some object of interest is a simple form of worship easily understandable by the children. Hymns and prayers and children's spontaneous remarks provide the setting in which it is easy to talk of God as our loving father, and make them familiar with stories of Jesus and particularly the Christmas story. The stories, however, should be the summary of the child's other activities rather than the reverse. Such subjects as Jesus' home; "the Lord God made them all", i.e. flowers, stars, animals; the House of Praise, i.e. the Church; care of animals, lend themselves to expression work well within the compass of infant children.

(ii) *Early Childhood*. "Learning by doing" is still the principle to remember with young children. Stories become real by acting rather than by listening, and the parables of Jesus are even better mimed than acted. The association of familiar things with the providence of God can have as its basis the procession of the seasons and the phenomena of nature. It was in these ways that the early Hebrews themselves first came to think of God, and there is a "moral" in the story that it is in the gentler manifestations of God— the "still, small voice"—that He comes to speak more intimately to men.

The daily life of Jesus and His times starting from a comparison with the child's own life and times will provide contrasts and similarities. There is no place for doctrine until very much later, and we have to be careful to recognize the child's natural limitations.   The presentation of abstract terms to be rehearsed and memorized far beyond any context of experience is a substitute for genuine growth in knowledge, even if it gives a bland satisfaction to the teacher, or, more properly, to the propagandist. A beginning should be made here with Old Testament stories in the form of "stories that Jesus would hear from His mother", as this avoids the awkwardness which the question "Is it true?" always brings when it follows stories such as " Noah's Ark" or the rainbow. Stories of "friends of Jesus", not only of His own time but later, down to our own day, follow on from the account of Jesus' own lifetime, and place will also be found for the presentation of the Church as an extension of the family.

(iii) *Later Childhood*. This period up to the age of eleven exhibits very much a transition from a concern for what is fanciful to concern with reality. Wordsworth's "shades of the prison house" are beginning to close round, or, alternatively and contrariwise, the child's horizon is becoming wider. It is noticeable that his fellows and his school are beginning to count more with him than his home, not because he despises home but because the settled security of home gives him a base from which he can venture without undue risk.

He can thus appreciate stories of action, particularly if there is plenty of characteristic detail. The Old Testament heroes and stories of martyrs and missionaries are particularly attractive, and the savagery of the primitive Hebrew fighters is often no more than an added attraction! The question of the truth of these stories is bound to arise, and the earlier treatment of this question will have to be supplemented by the clear distinction between history, myth and legend. This is a distinction that arises in other contexts as well as that of the Bible, and the teacher will have to make up his mind before the question actually arises. The place of prophecy in the Old Testament is important at this stage, especially as Jesus quoted so much from the prophets. Certain select Psalms can be introduced as part of the hymn book that Jesus used.

In the New Testament the central point of study should be the life of Jesus exhibited in a series of dramatic incidents followed by similar incidents in the life of Paul. At some point the worship of the school should be linked up with Biblical studies in personal religion, as, for instance, in the prayer-life of Jesus, but too much ought not to be expected of children at this stage. Religious education is a graded process and the results of earlier teaching often do not appear at all until years after, when the process of re-interpretation has begun.

(iv) *The stage of puberty* is, of course, marked by great physical and mental changes, although some children pass through it with very little difficulty. The characteristic institutions at this stage are the Boy Scouts and the Girl Guides, both of them organizations which make use of the strong sense of following a leader which children develop. A further characteristic is the development of self-conscious-ness and a sense of the seriousness of life. Once at a boys' camp at which I was an officer a group of us went for a walk and came to a ruined village. In the middle of the village was a disused well. One of the boys accidentally kicked a stone into it. With an unexpected sense of awe he solemnly said to a companion as they moved away, "Think of that stone being down there from now onwards for hundreds and hundreds of years".

This sense of time and timelessness is something that is carried forward into adolescence but it begins at this stage. Consequently children are prepared to listen to anything which stirs within them this primitive response. They are

also attracted by Christ as the leader and they can appreciate
His hard way of the Cross. The story of Jesus should now be
based on the study of a Gospel and the early chapters in
Acts. The real point of the Old Testament can now be made
clear by a study of one of the prophets, say Amos, in this
context, for here we have action, leadership and also the
sense that moral values do matter and are not just conventional.

(v) *Early Adolescence.* The stress and strain that are
characteristic of adolescents are largely due to a sense of
ineffectiveness in a world which they find ready made for them.
It is certainly not fashioned to their hearts' desire, it is domi-
nated by older people who assume or appear to assume that
the young people will accept the existing way of life without
question. The idealism of youth is partly a revolt against this
assumption, and is partly frustrated by it. But where there is
conflict there is also a recognition of moral and spiritual
values by which that conflict is to be judged.

It is a time of questioning, of experiment, of independence,
and yet at the same time, paradoxically, of a greater need
than ever for security. Susan Isaacs held that the great needs
of children were for security, affection and significance,
but she limited these to young children. They are, however,
needs of people at *every* age, and at none are they more marked
than in early adolescence. The hooliganism of young boys of
this age in our city streets is a symbol of their lack of satisfaction in these regards. The juvenile scepticism of grammar
school boys and girls is but another form of the same thing.

In what, therefore, is the religious education of children
at this stage to consist? It is a mistake so to organize a syllabus
that the later years are marked simply by an ever-increasing
amount of detail. A good many of the English Agreed
Syllabuses err in this regard. The earlier sections are admirably
done and well suited to the ages of the children for whom they
are intended. The later sections take on more and more the
aspect of a university syllabus. It is better in these matters
to attempt an elementary subject in an advanced way than to
do an advanced subject in an elementary way.

Consequently at this stage instead of *adding* to the content of the syllabus it is better to go back over what has been already done and seek to re-interpret it. *Genesis*, for example, has admirable material for the youngest children. But so it has for the fifteen-year-old. It is more a matter of freshness of method than freshness of content, although no doubt the content has to be increased as well. The parables of the Gospels are excellent story material for young children, but they were not told in the first instance to young children, nor were they told simply as stories. They therefore have a place in the teaching of older children who are able to appreciate the reasons why Jesus told them.

(vi) *Later Adolescence.* The contrast between the world as it is and the world as youth would like it to be is complicated at this point by a third element of contrast, namely, that with the world as it thinks itself to be. There is here a keen appreciation of the difference between the claims that persons or institutions make for themselves and their actual worth or performance. In our generation the violence of this contrast is such that disillusionment with things as they are is the characteristic attitude of young people all over the world. All the old slogans—"the war to end war", "making the world safe for democracy", "a land fit for heroes to dwell in"—had come to have a hollow sound long before World War II was upon us. The unnatural viciousness of Hitler's régime awakened people again to the values that were worth while and there was a more general response to the war against Hitler than to the war against the Kaiser. Survival itself seemed to be threatened.

And now, long after that victory was won and survival assured, we are trembling on the brink of World War III, but this time with great hosts of the youth of the world sympathetic to the enemy. Disenchantment with democracy and the belief that only the strong hand and the unopposed will can bring salvation to the nations is evident on every side. And even where youth does not approve of Communist totalitarianism it quite often embraces Roman Catholic totalitarianism in the belief that any sort of totalitarian régime is better than the fluctuating indecisions of popularly elected governments.

This is the modern picture. The main features, however, have been there for generations. Things as they are, things as they are thought to be and things as they ought to be are the perpetual concern of the later adolescent. The issues as often as not are evaded and people live for the immediate moment only, and nothing is more astonishing than the anæsthesia with which so many people can pass through crisis after crisis and be apparently untouched by and indifferent to them. Now the value of the Bible at this stage is that these three contrasting factors as well as the attitude of indifferentism to all of them are the very situation to which the Biblical message addresses itself. In a sense that is what the Bible is about, and to say that its central theme is redemption is to say that the central theme of all human life is redemption— redemption from sin and ineffectiveness to a full, free and effective life as a child of God, the heir of all the ages, or, to use Biblical language, the "heir of the promises".

This wrestling with circumstances and with conflicting wills and with innate tendencies to evil marks the passage into adult life of every person of character, and the "religious education" which we need at this stage is not propaganda on behalf of a specific creed but a recognition that man's life is a warfare upon this earth and woe betide the man who treats it otherwise. The centrality of the Cross of Christ for thought and action and its acceptance as a personal conviction must be the goal of all religious education that is Christian. But it is achieved not by indoctrination or by blind obedience to institutional leaders or by resting content with Biblical history and literature, but by some deep radical loyalty to Christ Himself. This alone is to arrive at maturity. The Biblical phrase is translated "perfection", a most unfortunate word which has given rise to a mostunfortunate theology of so-called "Christian perfection". But the Greek word τέλειος has no such ambiguity. It means "the measure of the stature of the fullness of Christ".[1]

1 Ephesians iv. 13.

CHAPTER VI

THE EDUCATION OF THE EMOTIONS:
(1) NATURAL RELIGION

I

A FAMOUS old book by Philip Doddridge is entitled *The Rise and Progress of Religion in the Soul*, and the theme if not the treatment of it is relevant to religious education.

We come into this world with a long history already behind us. Far beyond the ancient Britons and beyond *pithecanthropus erectus,* we descend or, if you will, we ascend from the earliest speck of life on this planet. In an unbroken succession the line has come down from the very fount of life, God Himself, who is the source of all things.

But this is not the only ancestry that we have. There is one that is more immediate. Every living person has this unbroken chain of ancestors reaching back through the aeons of time, but he has also an unerring sense of being a new creation, different from all others, not explainable in terms of his ancestors at all but coming direct out of the source of life itself. Where was I before I became what I am now? If, as some psychologists hold, there is a trauma of birth, the shock is caused not just by physical causes but by the contrast unconsciously experienced between that mysterious world of spirit from which we have come and the conditions of life here and now. There is no proof, of course, of any of this, but there is one line of experience which is suggestive, namely, "the rise and progress of religion in the soul".

> Trailing clouds of glory do we come
> From God Who is our home.
> Heaven lies about us in our infancy.

The sense of God comes to us as that of a power not ourselves making itself known in creation, in beauty, in conscience and in fear.   Sometimes it comes in darkness and terror,
in the piercing shriek of the hurricane, in the upheaval of a
mountain, in the horrors of plague, or in tragic changes of
fortune.   ''Fear created the gods'', said Statius, and this fact
was well accepted in the Middle Ages.   But there are other
manifestations of the unseen that are more kindly and gentle.
They steal upon us almost unawares in the experience of
human love, in the painful beauty of the setting sun, in moon-
light over the sea, in the sweetness of Mozart's music, or in
haunting appeal of a single line of poetry—

A rose-red city half as old as Time—

but in whatever way they come they authenticate the existence
of an unseen world of spirit with which at one and the same
time we have a sense of affinity and a sense of strangeness.
It is in this contact with nature in all its forms and the conviction of something over and above the evidence of the senses
that we have to look, in Dr. R. R. Marett's notable phrase,
for ''the birth of humility''.

When I consider thy heavens, the work of thy fingers,
The moon and the stars, which thou hast ordained;
What is man, that thou art mindful of him?

This psalm puts into a personal form an experience of which
everyone from the most primitive even to the most sophisticated has some knowledge.   It comes not only through nature
but also through beauty of every kind—of sight, colour, sound
and personal relationship.   It takes different forms in different
religions; sometimes it is expressed as abjectness and sometimes as exhilaration, but in every form it is a recognition
of the existence of something outside ourselves that is
''from everlasting to everlasting'', against which the life
of man is but a shadow.

This intuitive sense of God is, as we have seen, the beginning of religion, and like the growth of a tree this earlier

growth remains at the heart of every later development. Deep within all our different forms and revelations there is natural religion—the sense of God in nature and in the unsophisticated mind of man. The historical religions explain it, give it a name, criticize and discipline it, but they do not, and cannot, explain it away. The intellect is driven by this sense of the unknown to seek to make it known, and scientific curiosity is itself a witness to the mysteriousness of the universe. Pride takes hold of the intellect when it is cut off from this source, and men imagine that in their own thinking is the beginning of all science and all religion. This is a common theme of Greek tragedy, the pride of men in their own cleverness forgetting God, and also of primitive mythology, the giants that scale the heights of heaven and are hurled headlong "with hideous ruine and combustion".

This natural religion shows itself very strongly in the time of adolescence, for it is the biological changes of puberty and the pains of adaptation to modern society that bring the civilized man back to the experiences of primitive life. The interest of this period lies in the coincidence of primitive impulses and an informed modern curiosity. The adolescent is thus a good deal more primitive than the child. There is in his experience a sense almost of disintegration, sometimes pleasant, sometimes very painful, and objects of concern group themselves round three main feelings: the sense of the littleness of human life compared with the vast span of the ages and the incredible size of the universe; the sense of incompleteness and frustration in all experiences that are enjoyable; and the sense of the sacred as something which is at once overwhelming and attractive. These experiences are the raw material that is misused by Romanticism but they represent, so to speak, an outcrop of natural religion with which education is very vitally concerned.

Nevertheless, for the natural man this experience is one of contact with a world that is anonymous. He does not know with what or with whom he has to do. This anonymous Presence therefore needs to be given a name and the unseen world itself needs to be "informed", to be given form. This happened in the beginnings of history in folklore and mythology. The powers of nature were personified and familiarity drew the sting of their awfulness. But it has better come about through men's reflection on their own experiences, through the insight of persons particularly sensitive to spiritual qualities, such as the Hebrew prophets and the prophets and poets of every age and country, through the pattern that gradually shows itself in the history of the race, and through the accumulated records of the experiences of men in this sphere. Looked at from one side these have all been men's discoveries about the unseen world. From the other side they are God's revelation of Himself. In this sense, therefore, there is not and there never has been "religion without revelation". It is the same God who was there in the first nuclear fission whom we now believe to be "the father of our Lord Jesus Christ".

When, however, our own interpretation of the unseen world becomes so familiar that we cease to question it, a new problem arises.

A moral difficulty in the case of historical religions is that they express themselves in words so fully that God is apt to become narrowed down to the compass of our own thought. Hence arises that familiarity in the things of God which is the sin of idolatry; it is to worship that which our minds have made. From this spring all manner of censoriousness and superciliousness whether in doctrine or in morals. In this context clarity of thought is often the foe to humility. On the other hand, face to face with the natural universe, with the God of the bright sky or the storm cloud, of the mountain and the plain, a man feels his own littleness, and this natural religion is an integral part of the Christian religion and of Judaism. To the prophet Amos, the God who insisted that judgement should roll down as waters and righteousness as a mighty stream was the same God who made the Pleiades and Orion. The unknown prophet of the Exile reminds contemporaries that the God whom they appear to know so well is "he that sitteth on the circle of the earth and the inhabitants thereof are as grasshoppers". And Jesus Himself gave the same warning to those who light-heartedly take oaths: "the heaven is the throne of God and the earth is the footstool of his feet".

Now concentration in religious education on the historical and literary side of the Bible may expose people to precisely this temptation of familiarity. They may easily mistake religious knowledge for religion. An earlier generation valued knowledge mainly for its *form*: the present generation is apt to value it mainly for its *content*. Yet the alternative is not an authoritarian creed, for the authoritarian may be just as much the victim of his own intellect as the modernist: he is apt to be concerned with propositions intellectually conceived, and he is looking for certainty. The real alternative is to recognize that the goal of all our endeavour in religious education is to help a child to be at home in the universe, which is his Father's house, and to behave accordingly. This means natural religion interpreted and not superseded by Christianity, and a spirit to which all pettiness is alien and all self-seeking impossible.

2

Christianity, as we have noted, is one religion out of many, and so this natural religion of all men is something that includes Christianity within it. But the converse is equally true, namely that natural religion is included within Christianity, together with a great deal more. They are two circles that partly overlap so that part of each is contained within the other. In the course of history this mysterious power behind the universe has been revealed as a Person of a particular character, and as men have acted on the belief they have developed it still further. They have discarded certain views of God which have been found to be untrue to a higher revelation of His nature, and although in so doing they have often landed themselves into dilemmas, they have clung to the more ethical view of His character rather than to a more logical view in which there was no dilemma at all.

Christianity, therefore, contains much that is not present in natural religion. It is concerned with history, with human beings in fellowship with one another and with God Himself as these other factors reveal Him. It has a vision of human destiny and it impels towards action. It has, moreover, a standard of life in the person of Jesus Christ, and it is therefore present in the world not as a mere inevitable evolution from a primitive natural religion but as a perpetual challenge to things as they are. It recognizes the existence of dark forces of sin in oneself and in the world, and it has a gospel of deliverance. Natural religion is essentially conservative, Christianity is essentially revolutionary, but in so far as it includes natural religion it has a conservative element within it.

Accordingly we are continually witnessing a conflict between two views of Christianity: the one which looks upon religion as a stabilizing force in the State, the other which looks upon it as a call to action. These two views often correspond to differences in age; often they correspond to differences in social and spiritual security. In religious education in schools the school authorities may represent the former and the Sixth Form the latter, and it is no solution to the problem to tell the Sixth Form that when they are as old as the Chairman of the Governors they will have worked this revolutionary fervour out of their system. Nor is it a solution to identify this critical attitude with moral turpitude and to give conformity the colour of moral perfection. This is an avoidance of the real issue and an achievement of equilibrium at a low level.

Which side of religion is regulative? A. E. (George Russell) writes of "the dark churches where the blind mislead the blind" and holds to a religion of nature. Matthew Arnold and Swinburne would have agreed with him. Others— and not all of them Puritans—see the danger as well as the drift in a purely "natural religion" and would bring it all under subjection to the God of the Christian revelation.

The word "natural" is here ambiguous. Does it mean, as it meant with Rousseau, something primitive, intuitive, altogether away from books and institutions, morality and civilization? Or does it mean something that chimes in with man's nature? One of Benjamin Whichcote's aphorisms is that "nothing is more natural to man's soul than to receive truth". Is Christianity, therefore, conceivable as being "natural" to man, as natural as and indeed more natural than animism or any other primitive religion?

It is a fundamental fact of education that what is "natural" is the end rather than the beginning of the educational process. It is indeed the great achievement of education to reveal a man's real nature both to himself and to his fellows. At every stage education becomes more and more selective, sorting out, shall we say, science men from arts men, and then among the science men biologists from physicists, and then again among the biologists botanists from zoologists, always dividing and sub-dividing, until we arrive at that which is most characteristic and therefore most "natural" to the man himself. To believe that the natural is the primitive is to fall a victim to a chronological fallacy. In theology it is to assume that the nearer we get back to the time of the Apostles the nearer we are to the truth. The writer to the Hebrews did not believe in this principle. "God hath provided some better thing for us" than for our ancestors. The "natural" is that which is the essence of a thing, and the essence may take a long while to distil out.

Consequently the Christian Gospel will be found to contain and not to contradict anything that is of the true nature of man, no matter how early or how late it has made its appearance. The humanist dilemma, for instance, "thy sons, O Zion, against thy sons, O Greece",[1] may represent quite unreal alternatives. The contradiction may be true at this or that stage in the progress of mankind, or of an individual, or in this or that situation, but it cannot be universally true in a world in which God has revealed Himself in many ways.

[1] Zechariah ix. 13.

But it is as we move forward that we see more and more content in the Gospel, more of what it really is, and John Robinson, the Pilgrim Father, proclaimed a truth that is at the very heart of Christianity when he declared "God has yet more light and truth to show forth from his word". The "light and truth", however, is very often not something new but something very old which hitherto has been thought to have been at variance with or irrelevant to the Gospel. We hold with Aristotle that the real nature of a thing is shown in its highest manifestation, and this need not be its original form at all.

3

One important way, however, in which "natural" religion is a permanent and essential element in Christianity is that it is a school of manners. I have already spoken of "the birth of humility". Good manners are the manifestation of humility. To see oneself over against the whole process of creation, in the presence of God who is from everlasting to everlasting, is to begin to see life in proper perspective. The differences between mankind, between class and class, are infinitesimal compared with the difference between our ways and the ways of God. Of what, therefore, have we to boast as between man and man? Are we not all God's creatures and are we not all standing in the need of prayer? Is it not presumptuous, to say the least of it, to imagine that we can enclose God within our human categories, and, for example, proclaim *ex cathedra* the "sure and certain" will of God concerning mixed marriages or the status of the South African native—the will, that is to say, of God who was there before the earliest planet started on its journey around its sun, who dwells in light unapproachable, and in whom all things had their origin? That men can show such bland self-assurance is a stronger argument for the wilfulness of unredeemed human nature than the drunkenness of some poor sot who is unable to pass a public-house. Ambition, self-flattery, pride and all manner of uncharitableness inevitably follow from that assumption of infallibility which is the fatal disease of the Christian man. Against all this the sense of a God whose throne is in the heavens and the footstool of whose feet the whole earth is a very healthy corrective. "Manners makyth man", and the manners of Christ makyth the Christian man. There is no more pregnant story in the Bible than that of Jesus washing the disciples' feet—not because of the humility of the action itself but because of the reasons the author gives for it.

> Jesus, *knowing that the Father had given all things into his hands and that he was come from God and went to God* . . . began to wash the disciples' feet.

The sense of the majesty of God and of his over-ruling providence forms in the Christian that willingness to serve others which is the core of all good manners.

4

It is often taken as a matter of course that we are wiser than our fathers. We know more about the forces of nature and have greater control over them: we have at our disposal more material for understanding the history of the race and the nature of government, and we have better ways of using it.

And yet there appears to be something wrong. War has not vanished from the earth and its technique keeps pace with the marvels of applied science. Worse still, there are definite throw-backs to primitive savagery. Anti-Semitism has led in our times to an orgy of animal hate beside which the worst excesses of the Middle Ages were comparatively mild. Progress in education puts greater possibilities for good into the hands of the good, but also greater possibilities for evil into the hands of the evil.

Nor is it only the times that are out of joint. Our intellectual progress does not seem to touch the deepest problems

H

of the human heart. Sorrow, frustration, despair and sin are not less with us personally than they were with our ancestors, and the flight of time makes no difference.

What, therefore, is wrong with our education? How is it that all the progress in the world would appear to be simply progress in comfort and in the control of matter, and that the needs of persons are precisely the same as they always were? The more people know the more helpless they appear to be. Accordingly, social reformers and others turn upon our educational system and say all manner of evil concerning it. It is too competitive, it is class-ridden, the wrong subjects are studied, teachers need more training, we have too much of it, we need more of it, the school-leaving age needs to be raised.

These things may well be true, but they do not go down to the root of the matter. The truth is that education carries with it its own peculiar inherent difficulty which we cannot get rid of by any mere change in curriculum, or examinations, or system. Progress in education inevitably widens the gulf between thought and emotion and puts asunder that which God has joined together. We progress on the intellectual plane while standing still, or even receding, on the emotional. So much is this the case that everything becomes, so to speak, intellectualized, and intellectual values predominate. For a feeling we substitute the idea of a feeling, or even the name of a feeling; beauty becomes something not so much to be respected and enjoyed as to be analysed; even the most intimate human relationships are dissected into complexes and the like, and, in the apt phrase of Quiller-Couch, we are constantly "hanging up (without benefit of laundry) our common humanity as a rag on a clothes-line". All this is evident on the large scale, but it is equally true if we come down to the schools and the teachers. Intellectualism makes feeling impossible. Our emotions are left to take care of themselves, or they are cultivated altogether apart from our intellects, or they are simply rationalized away.

To compensate for this, non-academic subjects are often put into the curriculum—art, domestic science, scouts, summer camps—or use is made of the organization of the school itself—houses, prefects, fags, games, prizes. Often these aspects of life which are not "work" are credited with the formation of character—a task which is explained as a higher one than "work", especially if the examination results of the year have been none too good. The result is that our intellectual work is carried on by itself, it is usually sound and by the aid of intelligence tests is well graded; but meanwhile our cleverest boys and girls and young men and women may have an "emotional age" (if there could be such a thing) far behind their "mental age". There are even eminent scholars and well-known divines and thousands of hard-headed business men who are emotionally as immature as children.

This gap between thought and emotion has itself been the subject of discussion to the detriment of emotion. Emotion is considered to be a dangerous thing, something that needs discipline because of its connection with the physical side of our being, something primitive and hostile to intelligence. On the other hand, emotion may be looked upon as a higher category than thought, and we are urged to give way to it. This attitude is often taken by "arty" people, and by certain schools of religious practice. But both attitudes assume that emotion and thought are alternatives. So indeed they may be —at certain levels—but the aim of the education of the emotions is to keep them in close relationship, not allowing the one to predominate over the other or to take the place of the other. Once they are separated they are *each* of them capable of doing untold damage, and if it be true that emotion needs to be disciplined by thought, it is just as true, and indeed in these days more true, that thought needs to be disciplined by emotion.

There are certain characteristics of our emotional life which we must notice before we embark on a study of its education.

There is, first of all, its connection with physical life. Strong feelings are accompanied by exceptional physical conditions,—the staring eyes of fear, the reddened cheek of shame, the faster pulse of excitement and a good many others. Control over these physical signs may check the emotion, while exhibiting them may induce it. At the same time, and apparently in flat contradiction to this physical connection, is the fact that while it lasts an emotion transports us to a different stage of existence, sometimes lower, sometimes higher, but at any rate never ordinary. Why is it impossible to reason with a person in the grip of anger or fear? Because for the time being his reasoning power is inhibited and he is not susceptible to any argument. Any attempt to argue simply feeds the emotion by adding to it a sense of frustration, and is worse than useless. It is, therefore, particularly dangerous to manoeuvre a child, or indeed anyone, into a position where he becomes the victim of his own emotion. We must wait for the emotion to subside. If the person is alone in experiencing the emotion it will subside quickly, and once he has been able to look at himself and notice that he is gripped by emotion, the emotion will lose its hold and become a *thought* and can be dealt with as such. If, however, he is with other people who are in the grip of the same emotion, it is intensified and may result in action completely alien to the man's real nature.

Then again an emotion is a thrill and is enjoyable. Even fear has a strange fascination and men court it for the thrill it gives. The sensations of vastness and strangeness are both enjoyable. So also is the "sensational" novel or the cinema. Sex, perhaps, for many people is the most enjoyable experience of all, because so many things can be made to come together in the one situation—physical contact, the sense of abandonment, the sense of possession, the bliss of experiencing for the moment a timeless existence in which all life's ideals are fused together, and, on occasion, the possibility of wrong-doing and defiance of society. Sympathy is quite often an emotion. It is a very dangerous spiritual condition because it may actually lead to the creation of weakness and misfortune in order to have the thrill of sympathy. Sir Roger de Coverley tells the Spectator about the widow with whom he was in love: "How often have I wished her unhappy that I might have the opportunity of serving her".

This is a harmless example of a frame of mind which in base natures becomes cruelty in order to enjoy the thrill (which has a close connection with sex excitement) of sympathy with the victim.   Corporal punishment in school is sometimes an illustration of this fact.   It produces in a certain type of boy the thrill of abandonment to physical hurt, and in a certain type of teacher the thrill of a perverted sympathy for his own victim.   It is therefore bad for both, especially if it stimulates sex excitement.   It is noticeable how men and women of unstable temperament will pass rapidly from beating a child to caressing it.   Sympathy of this kind, and indeed of some other kinds also, is entirely self-centred; the other person is there not to be served but to serve.   Sometimes kindness is of this character: its purpose is to give a glow of satisfaction to the person who is being kind.   The relationship between growing girls is often of this self-centred type, masquerading as a concern for the other person.

Finally, an emotion is an impulse to action—that is what the word itself means.   If it is a feeling of repulsion it calls for some action to remedy what is wrong; if it is one of attraction it still requires action of some kind.   If we are pleased with a landscape we find ourselves calling to someone else, "Oh, look at that view!"   When strong emotion is frequently aroused without being followed by action, this can lead to a morbid condition.   Hence come sentimentality concerning the feeling when it is present, and the craving to "work up" feeling when it is not there—neither of them healthy attitudes but both of them all too common where the emotions have not been educated.

5

Let us now consider ways in which we can educate the emotions and bridge this gap between emotion and thought.

An emotional state is one of absorption, and the more it

is associated with other sides of life the longer will that absorption be present. Emotions are sudden and momentary, but an emotional state, a feeling, involves more than a mere response to a stimulus. It is a fusion of thought and will into one condition of satisfaction or frustration. To be absorbed in the music at a concert is to be oblivious of everything outside, not hearing the clock or noticing that the room is getting dark. But the feeling is more than a mere delight in sounds—it involves discrimination between sounds, an ear for harmony, perhaps some knowledge of the pieces played, perhaps also a strong conviction that this is a better way than any other of spending your time. The psychologists, who have their own way of talking about things, call this "the building up of an emotion into a sentiment", and a sentiment is a more permanent condition than an emotion. Moreover, it works conversely as well, and to be in touch with the non-emotional elements in a sentiment—for example, to read in the paper that there is to be a concert in a fortnight's time or to hear that Beethoven's house in Bonn is in danger of destruction—will stimulate the sentiment into life and with it recall the feeling.

This linking of a feeling with intellectual elements is a way of educating it, deepening it and making it part of, instead of an escape from, normal life. Without such a link the feeling is simply a momentary thrill, the enjoyment of which drives the person to seek to have another of the same kind. But a thrill when repeated is less of a thrill, and if repeated often it ceases to be a thrill at all. It requires the showman's "bigger and better" sensations in order to reproduce the same intensity of emotion. Hence there is no real satisfaction to be got from a succession of thrills, for there must come a point at which no further increase of sensation is possible, and to leave a person to seek the satisfaction of his emotions in this way is to make his emotional life very precarious indeed. It keeps the emotions at the same low level, not keeping pace at all with intellectual development and even, in the case of many people, making intellectual development impossible, for it centres the real interest of life on these moments of excitement.

This association of thought and emotion has a very important bearing on religion, for in the case of Christianity religious feeling cannot be mere emotion—since feeling, although the most "religious" element in Christian experience, is, as we have seen,[1] only one element out of five, all of which are concerned in the full Christian way of living.

Yet while the association of feeling with the other sides of life creates a more permanent state, it has certain difficulties. It makes the emotion itself more and more hard to reach. The momentary emotion is a response to a stimulus, and if we can produce the right stimulus, the response will come. But a "sentiment", while it makes it possible to recapture the first fine careless rapture, also means that the emotion is no longer near the surface or easily accessible. The simpler and cruder emotion is inhibited, but on the other hand the emotion that does ultimately emerge from a deeper level is a far more satisfying experience, because it covers so much more of a man's life. People are not always willing to take this trouble—they like their thrills quick and snappy, and even intellectual people often value most the kind of emotion that is non-intellectual.

Rationalizing an emotion destroys it at that level, and to have the habit of thus rationalizing everything is to make emotion impossible. There is, of course, a good side to this because it destroys anti-social and morbid emotions as well as good ones, and it is indeed one way of dealing with them. To explain a person to himself and to get him to accept the explanation does not make him a saint, but it makes him aware of what is happening if he insists on being a sinner. More people than we think are surprised into doing wrong instead of deliberately setting out to do it, and this is particularly the case with adolescents. To build up awareness, therefore, is to do a useful service, although only a negative one.

[1] pp. 14 ff. above.

Nevertheless, the difficulty remains. The habit of awareness presents us with both sides of a question, and we may
keep on looking at them. It is this sort of attitude which in
the end inhibits action altogether, because it takes away the
power to act. As we say, "we have no strong feelings either
way".

What, then, are we to do for the education of the
emotions in a context such as this? We need by example and
precept to show people that action is impossible unless one
side or the other is definitely rejected. The theory that truth
always lies in the middle is itself untrue and it leads to the
ignoring of plain issues. It has not needed Kierkegaard to tell
us that truth is discoverable only where there is decision;
until we make up our minds and proceed to action no moral
issue has been faced at all. The rejection of one side, or the
rejection of what we conceive to be two extremes, does not
always mean a choice between good and bad, it quite often
is the much more difficult decision between good and very
slightly better. Choice in this case *looks* as if it were approving
the one and condemning the other, but this is the price we
have to pay for action.

Let me take a very frequent example of this. Does not
a man's choice of a denomination imply a censure on all the
others which he has not chosen? This is certainly how it
appears, but the risk has got to be run. And the strange thing
is that he will never discover the truth that is in any unless
he definitely and loyally makes up his mind about *one*. Loyalty
to one particular group combined with perfect courtesy in
thought as well as in manner to members of other groups is
the basis on which men of goodwill come together. The
same problem arises about political parties. The best
"mixers" in the House of Commons are the convinced but
also courteous party men. It arises also about vocation—and
so often people try to follow hybrid vocations in order to
avoid choosing between two that are equally good. It is
only by making a choice, and thereby apparently throwing

away all the marks of an educated and balanced judgement, that we recapture the emotion of self-abandonment to a cause that is larger than ourselves. Thus the understanding and the practice of one religion is a better religious education than a study of "comparative religion" undertaken under the mistaken idea that you are thereby giving all religions a fair chance and are being broadminded.

There is need, therefore, to get at emotion *through* the intellect and not as an alternative to it. Fortunately this is quite possible, for although intellectual awareness inhibits emotion at one level, it is discoverable again as the culmination of the intellectual process itself and on a deeper, more appropriate and more satisfying level. The goal of every intellectual process is feeling. The intellectual effort, however, has to go on not only long enough but also long enough *at a time* in order to get to the stage of complete absorption. The drudgery of striving is rewarded by vision. Indeed the truth of anything is never *only* the conclusion drawn from evidence: it is in the last resort a revelation, and the person feels it to be such. He may not conduct himself like Archimedes when the full truth of the principle of specific gravity burst upon him, but his attitude will be an emotional one, nevertheless. Hence the intellectual effort leads finally to a venture of faith: it carries us a good long way, but it cannot by itself carry us all the way. There comes at the end a flash of illumination—something not alien to the effort but arising out of it.

It is a curious thing, for example, how so often a rehearsal of a play seems so bad and the performance itself turns out to be so good. The lines have all been learned—and what a drudgery it is!—but at the end something happens and they are felt and not merely recalled. There is not much fun in doing French grammar, or the multiplication table, or endless routine experiments in physics, but these labours lead us to the place where insight becomes possible and the subject is experienced and no longer "learned". A real education of the emotions, therefore, consists in doing something which seems the very opposite, namely, prolonging the intellectual effort with greater thoroughness and greater faith.

There are two reasons why this experience so rarely comes. The first is that people give up long before that moment arrives. The other reason is that they confuse all this drudgery with learning. These last are the intellectual navvies of our schools and colleges, always quarrying but never building. Old John Earle, who published *Microcosmographie* in 1629, knew the type well. Of "a plodding student" he writes, "He hath a strange forced appetite to learning, and to achieve it brings nothing but patience and a body". It is perhaps not quite so bad as this, but school examinations, the quantitative view of knowledge and the present fashion of "research" all tend to exalt mere intellectualism and make people content to remain in that intermediate stage which is occupied with learning and not with mastery. There is a strangely impersonal atmosphere about this, and a sense of indiscipline hangs over it all. The pagans, suckled in a creed outworn, thought of truth as a goddess to whom one gave personal loyalty. It was only a picture, but it was nearer the mark than the view of truth as an absolutely irrefutable syllogism or a basketful of facts.

6

"Studies," said Bacon, "serve for delight, for ornament, and for ability." This attitude to study was characteristic of the leisurely days of the seventeenth and eighteenth centuries, when a few men could ponder over two or three large folios a year, but the nineteenth century altered all that and made studies serve for getting on in the struggle for life. "Knowledge is power" was another aphorism of Bacon which chimed in much better with the ideas of a later age. Consequently education has become concerned not so much with the person himself as with his position in society, and from being general and humanistic it has become more specific. Indeed, it is often referred to not as education at all but as "training". Specific abilities rather than general attitudes are cultivated.

We must therefore recognize the need to discipline the corrosive intellect. This, of course, is no discovery; the dispute arises as to how it is to be disciplined. It is commonly held that it must be disciplined by authority. The emotions are to be disciplined by thought, and thought is disciplined by authority. "Authority", however, means so many different things. There is the authority of the leader of an orchestra who is willingly accorded control over other people because they are only too glad to recognize that he stands supremely for something in which they believe, and is thereby representative of them. The authority of any person who is a master of some branch of knowledge or some craft is similarly due to his representative character. The authority of an institution may be quite different, due only to its ability to enforce (within its own bounds) its own will. But if you hold one opinion and I hold another and I am able to coerce you, I am not really affecting your opinion one way or the other. There is no discipline of the intellect in this. Indeed, it is worse, for insistence on infallibility in matters of opinion is but the other side of the medal to scepticism,[1] and results either from a fear that truth is unable to take care of itself, or more simply from pure conceit. This insistence has been found chiefly among churches, but is not unknown among scientists and statesmen.

The true discipline of the intellect comes from the emotions. One form of this discipline is to pursue the intellectual effort far enough till it takes fire. Another is to keep feelings and thinking constantly together except in those limited regions such as mathematics, where thinking alone is a sufficient instrument. For example, it may be that "planning" an educational system is a good thing, but to plan it without regard to the idosyncrasies of the people for whose benefit it

[1] See below, chapter IX.

exists is to produce a bad plan, no matter how excellent it is theoretically. In the case of schoolboys and girls with whom feeling is strong it is well to have that feeling disciplined by action and by thought, but it is equally important for them to realize in their intellectual activity that where human beings are concerned (as they are in all "humane" studies, and not in those alone) human feelings, including their own, are relevant to the issue. "Contempt of Thy word and command-ment" often arises in those who have contempt for those simple people whose intellects are not quite so subtle as are their own.

But here arises that peculiar condition of the intellect to which I have already referred (p. 100). It is the disease which we might call "nominalism" for it results in substitut-ing for an emotion the name of the emotion. This substitution is not uncommon in adolescence, although it is the copyright of no particular age, and its most usual form is romanticism. There are things in life which are good to have, but which lose a measure of their goodness as soon as you are aware that you have them. Love of nature and of people can be deepened by contacts and by education, but they are ruined as soon as they become a cult. Awareness of the love of beauty not only takes the place of the love of beauty itself but also brings a sense of superiority and Pharisaism which is one of the least lovely things in the world. Familiarity with romantic literature may absolve us from having the actual emotions with which it deals.

When this self-consciousness is found in an attitude to persons as well as to things it can work most deadly havoc. There is a word of which the Germans are very fond, *Welt-schmerz,* the sense of the sorrows of the world. Those who really have it talk about it least. These are the people who are wounded for our transgressions even when by their stripes we are not healed. But that is not what is usually meant by *Weltschmerz.* It usually means a self-conscious, Byronic attitude to life, romanticism masquerading as compassion. It can be found perfectly well in company with cruelty and lust and, indeed, as we have seen, may even be caused by cruelty as well as being a cause of it—a dualism not unknown even in the Church and one of the factors in religious persecution. Yet it is an extension of a very common and subtle confusion, that between a thing itself and the name of the thing. With such an attitude there can be no compromise, and in religious education particularly it must be recognized that pity and love in the ordinary, domestic and pedestrian sense are the real levers that have lifted us up from the beasts, rather than opinions about pity and love.

7

The last element in the education of the emotions is that which I would sum up under creative activity and the appreciation of it in others.

To have something that is one's very own, especially if we have created it ourselves, is one of the greatest thrills in life. Every child ought to have some private possessions which are not to be taken away from it even when it misbehaves. In the same way children like to have some legitimate secrets of their own which should not be subject to the prying eyes of adults. Even privacy is a right to which every child ought to be able to lay claim at some times in the day in his own home, and even in his own school, especially as he is growing older. All these things, possessions, secrets and privacy, are illustrations of the working out in childhood of the chief primitive drive of life, namely the insistence on being on top of one's own circumstances. These things help to educate the emotions by bringing a feeling of being treated as a "person" on one's own, with all the rightful sense of satisfaction and self-respect that follows from it.

But above all things it is in creation that we most express ourselves. Froebel, that wise teacher, used to say, "God creates, therefore I must create". To be a creator is to have a sense of personal worth and dignity which nothing else can bring. It is a different kind of achievement from that of merely overcoming a difficulty or carrying out a certain allotted task. It means bringing into existence something which but for you would not have been there at all. It is in this activity that a person is most characteristically himself. Yet the actual creation may be of very little consequence in the eyes of other people. I once interviewed a rather colourless student, and found it difficult to get out of him anything more than just "yes" or "no". I finally asked him what his hobbies were. He said he had none, but I could not believe it, and after a little persistence he stammered out that he collected match-boxes! I was so astonished at this hobby of a youth of twenty-one that I said that that would not take him very long. "Oh, wouldn't it?" he said. "Do *you* know how many kinds of match-boxes there are in the world?" I hazarded a hundred. "A hundred!" he said scornfully. "There are *thousands,* and I've got fifteen hundred of them." With this he became voluble and at last showed himself to be a person.

Creation, however, usually means more than collecting. It means overcoming resistance of some kind—not a resistance external to the situation, artificially brought in by school-masters and writers of text-books, but a resistance in the material itself. Woodwork for this reason is a better school craft than metalwork, because there is a grain in wood which has to be respected, and it is not until you know how to treat the grain that you can do anything.

Building up a friendship is also a creative activity, and there is a "grain" to be observed here too. This is a matter to which not a great deal of attention is given, and yet it is something on which a great deal of adolescent happiness depends. The type of highly emotional friendship that is found often in girls' schools and not so often (and yet still occasionally) in boys' schools, is unhealthy because it is self-centred. It is concerned not so much with regard for the other person as with *the idea of* regard for the other person.

Just as people are often in love with love, and the particular object (the word "object" is significant) of their affections does not really matter, so, too, with friendship. Moreover, such a friendship is often a victimization of the other person: it is a strain, a limitation of freedom, a relationship that is so lightly balanced that any trifle upsets it—in other words, it is a thoroughly morbid condition.

Some people's kindness is of the same nature. One test of the value of personal relationships is whether they make *both* parties feel stronger or weaker as a result. They cannot be perfect where one is strong at the other's expense or where both are weaker. There is a certain austerity necessary in friendship for it to be a success, and it is at its best where the friendship results not from the mutual interest of two people in one another but from a common loyalty to a cause or even to a third person. To be continually concerned about one's own feelings is to bid good-bye to all happiness in personal relations. They are made healthy by a strong measure of objectivity, for this is the ingredient that makes the relationship a new creation.

When we turn to appreciation of creative work we are in a region very familiar to the schools of today. Appreciation lessons in poetry, music, art and everything else are very common, and few there be who can do them well! For they are concerned both with study and with the pupil's own original effort. Originality depends upon an appreciation of other people's work. Novelists are usually diligent readers of novels, and poets of poetry. One reason why children produce so little of what is called "original" work is that they are given so little grist to their mill. They have nothing to be original *about*. Conversely, original work is a help in appreciating creative work. Froebel wanted his children to create in order that they might appreciate God's creation. And to have gone even a little way along the road trodden by the great poet or scientist or artist is to arrive at a position to appreciate his achievement. Sir Hugh Allen, when conductor of the Oxford Bach Choir, used to say, "Whatever is worth doing is worth doing badly!"

Education of the emotions through beauty comes from an appreciation of *wholeness*. A work of art is conceived whole, and the beauty of a view rests not in the details. Education is naturally analytical—it teaches people to see more and more distinctions and lays bare structure and process, the "what" and the "how", but if this is all there is to it, it has achieved but half its work. There must be a place somewhere for the sense of the whole to burst upon one. It may be at the beginning, when one's first impression is that of uncritical delight—as it is when seeing a gorgeous sunset. Or it may be at the end, as it is, for instance, in a detective story when the last page turns a collection of bits and pieces into a finished whole.

Accordingly, this kind of education depends not on analysis but on plentiful opportunities of seeing and hearing the best. They need to be unhurried and they need the minimum of explanation. The only real way to appreciate music is to hear it. It is by having the opportunity of hearing the same thing over and over again that you become "musical", rather than by acquiring a liking for those analytical concert programmes which—for all but the expert—get in the way of enjoyment. It is the same with pictures and with great literature. Even words and phrases can give an emotional delight, and quite small children of their own free will can in this way appreciate purple passages in literature as *sounds*, the meaning coming later. One of the most soul-stirring phrases that a certain small boy ever knew, and which never failed to thrill him, was taken from an advertisement in the London Underground. Beneath a picture of the inside of the power-station at Lots Road, Chelsea, were these words:

> These turbines sleep like tops, and out of their sleep comes the power to move London.

The boy who feels like that will also get a thrill out of Jeremiah:

He hath made the earth by his power, he hath established the world by his wisdom, and by his understanding
hath he stretched out the heavens. When he uttereth
his voice there is a tumult of waters in the heavens, and
he causeth vapours to ascend from the ends of the earth;
he maketh lightnings for the rain and bringeth forth the
wind out of his treasuries.

8

The education of the emotions, therefore, is a most
important aspect of education into religion. Because religion
is primarily feeling—a sense of the existence of the unseen
world with which we have to do—religious experience is
akin far more to æsthetic experience than to intellectual
processes. A historical religion, however, is concerned with
intellectual qualities which somehow have to be related to
this feeling. In Judaism and in Christianity, moreover, there
are not only the elements of feeling and knowing but also
the demand for standards—"Choose ye this day whom ye
will serve". In Christianity there is furthermore a loyalty
to a person, Jesus Christ, a relationship which not only
requires love and discipline and action (all of them concerned
with emotion) but brings with it a Gospel of deliverance
from the power of sin. It finds its sphere of action through a
society which is more than a group of like-minded people, for
it is the means whereby this Gospel is made known to the
present-day world.

Religion, like art, is concerned with wholeness, and as
that wholeness is something spiritual, it is in the last resort
only spiritually discerned. The factors of historical knowledge, doctrine and organization all count, and they all help
to deepen the religious feeling; but they do not provide it,
nor are they a substitute for it. Anything, therefore, which
makes us more acclimatized to that region of informed
thought and feeling is of service to religion. It helps to prepare the spirit of man to be at home in the universe which

I

is his Father's house. It also relieves religion of that photographic hardness which is characteristic of so many of its manifestations, and it fills it with colour and living interest. In the end of the day religion is concerned with what God does rather than with what we do, but to understand what He does needs a sensitiveness of spirit which arrives in only two ways, either by a cataclysmic conversion which affects temperament as well as morals, or by education. The education of the emotions is thus a preparation for the Gospel.

CHAPTER VII

STANDARDS

1

WHAT more is there in religious education than Bible teaching? One very common answer to this question is that morality or conduct is an essential part of the religious attitude and therefore moral teaching must be included. Nearly half a century ago there was published a large two-volume report on "Moral Teaching in Schools", in which moral teaching was treated as something apart from and almost as a substitute for religion. It is doubtful whether such a book could be published nowadays. We should now treat "morality" either as something arising out of religion and part of it or else as the code of manners prevailing at the time. During wartime in many countries "morality" came to mean that which was of most immediate benefit to your country. It might and did involve stealing from the enemy, lying, deceiving and murdering. After a few years of this sort of conditional morality it has proved exceedingly difficult to set up a code which applies to friend and foe alike.

From the point of view of morality, religion may be looked at from two quite opposite angles: it may be as a sanction in support of, or as a challenge to, the existing order, whether domestic, social or political. According to our acceptance of either point of view, so will be our religious education.

2

Religious education as a sanction is by far the commonest attitude. Hannah More looked upon religion as a method of keeping the "lower orders" content with their lot. It was

the perfect prophylactic against strikes.[1]   Samuel Wilderspin
believed that religious education was the cure for juvenile
delinquency.[2] Methodists have been heard to repeat Augustine
Birrell's quite unprovable judgement that the Methodist
Revival saved England from the horrors of a French Revolution.   There are many of our British contemporaries who
think that religious education will vaccinate our people against
Communism, while many Americans feel that a sound religious
training will strengthen people in their faith in private
enterprise.   None of these positions is really religious; they
are prudential and political and are concerned with keeping
things as they are.   The maintenance of the existing structure
of society is identified not only with good morality but also
with the will of God.

Nevertheless the fact that moral and religious teaching
should have this conservative aspect is an indication of something very deep and primitive in the soul of man.   If etymolo-
gically the word "religion" has its root in "*ligare, to bind*",
this too is its psychological justification.   In primitive society
and even in societies not so primitive, religion was the cement
that bound society together.   Augustus recognized the need
for it in the early days of the Roman Empire, and Hitler and
the Japanese warlords in our own time sought a religious
sanction for their régimes.   But private individuals as well
as rulers have recognized the urge to be on the right side of
deity in all transactions.   Taboos are simply the rules which
enable you to do this.   You say the right words, do the
appropriate actions, and henceforward your conduct has the
seal of heaven upon it.   However wilful or sinful a man may
be, he feels that for his own peace of mind he must so ration-
alize his sin or his wilfulness that it can appear to have divine
approval.   He acts as a person under authority even though
that authority may have no existence save in his own imagina-
tion.   That religion in the moral sphere is a collection of
"don'ts" is often urged as a criticism of the Old Testament

---

[1] J. L. and B. Hammond. *The Town Labourer 1760-1830*, pp. 225-30.
[2] The Infant System (1833). Chapter 3.

and of Victorian Protestantism.   In fact it is rooted in the heart of man, and "Thou shalt not" is the oldest form in which the moral sanction of religion makes itself felt.

We shall therefore not do justice to the spirit of man if we ignore this conservative and restraining aspect of religion. It is not the whole story, of course, but it is there both at the beginning of the story and at the end.   It begins in fear lest God should harm us and it ends in fear lest we should harm Him, and in both cases it keeps a rein upon the natural appetites.   Sin brings punishment in its train and we wish to ward off that punishment.   But sin also grieves God and we would not have that happen.   Religion, therefore, as a sanction brings with it this kind of negative morality.   For children in early stages as well as for the mature Christian it means discipline and submission to rules which are some-times laid down by others, sometimes laid upon oneself and not always either self-explanatory or even reasonable.   It is for lack of recognition of this side of religion that people grow up into an easy optimism about their own failings as well as about the pains and struggles of the world.   A religion which centres round the Cross of Christ cannot but be disciplinary in its very essence.

In the practice of religious education it is at this point that the false theory of "transfer of training" makes its appearance. As we have seen, however, there is no necessary carry-over from the learning of words to the practice of morality, and the assumption that there is is a plain misunderstanding of the whole learning process.   The schools, however, are not the only victims of this theory: it is widespread among all people who are concerned about morality.   The idea that words apart from the context of life have a meaning leads to that laziest of all types of evangelism, the "wayside pulpit" or the displayed text at railway stations.   These words may no doubt now and again startle with their aptitude a reader whose mind has already been dealing with the problem suggested, but it is the context and not the text that is the important thing.   Words without contexts are useless except to bring to a focus influences that are already there. In the case of Christian propaganda there is always the interpreting community to supply a context, but the mere moralist has no such support.

3

Religion as a sanction is characteristic of primitive and unprogressive societies and of the conservative mind everywhere. It is the most deeply rooted of all the religious types and, as we have seen, is invoked equally by dictators and by ordinary citizens. Religion as a challenge, however, is a peculiar product of Judaism and Christianity. Both these religions are concerned with the ideal and its achievement and are not content with things as they are. They share with other religions an element of conservatism, but it is their deep concern with history and with events and above all it is their essentially incarnational ethics that are the sources of their challenge to human life. The fact that truth is always conceived by them as something inherent in persons rather than in propositions, that it is something concerning life all round and something alive and growing, means that there is always tension in every human situation, and if it is not there, these religions will create it. The challenge, therefore, is not the call of a vested interest for its own self-preservation or aggrandisement. It is a challenge which is always to be found in every human situation and it cannot be ignored. The classic case is that of Jeremiah, who hated being in opposition to his fellow-countrymen, but the divine challenge to his generation was in him as a fire in his bones so that he "could not stay".[1] It is a challenge to the challenger himself and unless he meets it himself he is disqualified from passing it on to others in the name of Christianity. This is the beam that is in the eye of the man who first seeks to remove the mote from his brother's eye.

[1] Chapter xx. verse 9.

In religious education, therefore, it is the challenge even more than the sanction that has to be presented. Religion as a sanction is often made use of by the man himself for his own purposes to justify to himself actions and attitudes taken up on quite other grounds. It is against this form of rationalization that children and others have to be warned. Vices do not become virtues because they are indulged in the name of religion. Nothing is more clear in the New Testament than that the end does *not* justify the means. There is always held out before us the condemnation not only of those who said "Lord, Lord" and did nothing more about it, but also of those who "prophesied in thy name and in thy name did many mighty works" but were cast out with the terrible judgement "Depart from me, ye workers of iniquity". There is no law of compensation within the Christian life and no substitution. Earnestness in private and public devotion does not make up for irritability in the home or unwillingness to bear another's burden. This is a lesson that many mature Christians never seem to learn. It is not unknown, for instance, that attendance at a church committee has been held to justify sending in a bill for expenses in excess of the real figure. Zeal for orthodox doctrine permits a man to hate his neighbour if he thinks his neighbour is not orthodox. Wholeness of life is the only way in which to meet the challenge of Christian morality.

4

What, then, is the morality which depends on wholeness of life? Obviously it must be more than a maxim or even a principle. In my earliest schooldays, which happened at a time when religious education first came under the Cowper-Temple clause[1], it was discovered that moral teaching could be combined with training in good handwriting! Accordingly

[1] In the Education Act of 1870 and re-enacted in 1944. It lays down that in religious teaching in the grant-aided schools nothing distinctive of any denomination should be taught.

in copy-books called "Jackson's Upright System of Penman-ship" there was set at the head of each page in beautiful script such maxims as "Honesty is the best Policy" (a motto in which prudential considerations clearly have priority over moral ones) and "Waste not, Want not", each of which had to be copied eight or more times. The continual writing of these words in the book was expected to write all these laws in our young hearts.

Unfortunately there are two objections to this simple device. First, of course, it once more involves the fallacious theory of transfer. Secondly it is extremely doubtful whether men have as a matter of fact ever acted under the stimulus of any such copy-book maxims. There is something decidedly unhuman about a theory that all the magnificent integrated forces which make up human personality can be set going by no greater stimulus than the sight of sentences in a copy-book. Yet by many people this has most surely been believed. No doubt this provides an external standard by which to measure actions after they have taken place. Honesty and thrift are not difficult to discern as effects, but as motives they are in need of reinforcement.

A good deal depends on what we understand by excel-lence. Is it merely conformity to some rule or is it a quality of life which commends itself to the admiration and loyalty of those who behold it? Does it reside in an abstract idea or is it an external form, or is it best conceived in personal terms? Does it manifest itself from within, outwards, or can it be imposed from without, whether there is an inward response or not? These questions have only to be asked for the answer to appear along with the question.

In religious education use must therefore be made of the fact that it is not ideas or principles that people tend to follow but persons. They look round for the representative leader. And this is true also to the genius of Christianity. The Christian conception of excellence, as also the Christian conception of truth, is to be seen not in a logical system but in a person, and loyalty to a person rather than acceptance of a principle is the spring of Christian morality. No doubt there is danger in this. Loyalty to a person does not rule out variety nor personal initiative, and among those loyal to the same person there may be little in common save only that loyalty, but it is a strong enough bond of union if men will only allow it to be so. Everything depends upon the character of the person calling out that loyalty, for the nature of following a leader is essentially not mere conscious imitation of externals but a process of substitution. It is the gradual, almost unconscious, acceptance of someone else's way of life. The Pauline phrase is an exact one—"until Christ be formed in you". St. Augustine in a famous indiscretion, quite at variance with so many of his other writings, meant the same thing when he said "Love God and do as you like", for if you truly love God when you do "as you like" you will be doing as *He* likes, and here is the real check on antinomianism.

Nevertheless the danger remains. People interpret loyalty in different ways. One may believe that loyalty demands his passionate adherence to the two-nature theory of the person of Christ. Another believes that it means loving your neighbour and doing good as Jesus did, and that any dogmatic views of Christ's person are actually a stumbling-block if not an impertinence. The risk, however, has to be accepted. The real stumbling-block is not this or that theory but a self-centred attitude to life. There is nothing more flattering to the human soul or more productive of self-centredness than the sense of exclusive acquaintance with the unseen God. It is this and not any recognizable evidence that keeps going sects both great and small. To be able to stand up against all the divinity faculties of all the free universities of the world and assert that you alone have the truth about the Bible or about the Church or about divorce or about religious education is psychologically exhilarating and the thrill may easily be mistaken for contact with truth itself.

It is this attitude which inspires so many queer sects to interpret Hebrew prophecy with no greater *apparatus criticus* than their own uninformed English intelligence. It is this

attitude in another context which led the Roman Catholic
Bishop of Salford to lay down that

> Parents sending their children to non-Catholic schools
> when Catholic schools are available cannot receive Holy
> Communion. The clergy have been asked to report cases
> of parents causing scandal or irreverence to the Blessed
> Sacrament in this way.[1]

This way of interpreting Christian loyalty is very difficult for
the outsider to understand, for it seems to have little or
nothing to do with the Jesus of the New Testament. So, too,
was an "act of reparation" recently performed in London
to console Almighty God because the trustees of the Albert
Hall had let the building for a conference of the Rationalist
Press Association. These are vestigial survivals of more
primitive attitudes and their advantage is that they are easy
to adopt for oneself and easy to teach to others. Morality
as a code of regulations has about it that fixity of subject
matter which facilitates indoctrination, but education, and
particularly religious education, requires something quite
different.

There are stages in moral growth just as there are changes
in loyalties. To the young child a beloved parent or teacher
is the earliest example of "morality". The standard of conduct is what the older person approves or exemplifies. To
this extent the character of the teacher of religion is as important as his knowledge of the Bible or his expertness in teaching
it. It is not, as is so often assumed, a substitute for teaching
ability, but in its own sphere—i.e. that of moral training—
it is the required qualification, just as in another sphere a
thorough knowledge of the historical method is the required
qualification. Children will in any case become attached to
persons, and there is no harm in this provided that the persons
take it not as a personal compliment to be enjoyed but
as a golden opportunity to be wisely used. And it is rightly
used if it leads to an appreciation of those universal qualities

[1] Reported in *The Universe*, August 31st, 1951.

of moral character which presumably the admired person believes in and illustrates. We live by admiration as well as by hope and love.

It is obvious that there can be local loyalties—those which are sectional and incapable of leading to anything further. Accordingly part of religious education consists in leading children and adults also from purely local loyalties to an attachment to persons of greater and greater universal significance whether local or not. There is a gradation in heroes! A great mountaineer may be appreciated at one stage because he climbed Everest—a form of heroism scarcely open at all to any of his boyish admirers. But this mountaineering skill happens to be found along with the very effective witness of a Christian missionary—which represents a quality of life open to everybody. Hence he becomes appreciated at a later stage of growth as a Christian even more than as a mountaineer, and so the loyalty is extended. The only proper goal, however, of this extended loyalty is for it to be fixed upon the person to whom the hero too is loyal, namely, Christ Himself.

This integral association of moral qualities with persons is quite fundamental in religious education. Yet all such education is in danger from both the intellectual and the emotional side.

Undue emphasis on the emotions alone easily becomes sentimentality and undue emphasis on the intellect alone leads to sophistication. Both of these states of mind are tainted with nominalism. People fall in love with love instead of with a person, or they become concerned with "humanity" instead of with Tom, Dick and Harry. It is the romantic state of mind so very frequent in adolescence. The proper balance between thought and feeling has here been lost and is only adequately restored when principles are seen incarnated in persons and persons are appreciated both for their own sakes and also as representative of principles. There is a notable lack of generalization in the Gospels. Jesus deals with people as they come and according to their individual need. The rich young ruler is bidden to get rid of his riches, but Nicodemus is told to get rid of his sophistication. There is no generalization here about poverty or simplicity. He is dealing always with people and not with ideas about people.

5

On what grounds, therefore, do we attach ourselves to persons? We may be attracted to people because of their manners, their personal services to ourselves, their good fellowship, their strength of character, their optimism, or for many another reason. But we will not become their loyal followers, feeling an increased dignity in our very service of them and of what they stand for, unless somehow they represent something vital within us better than we can represent it ourselves. They are what we ourselves would willingly be if only it were possible. But it is far more than emulation, for emulation happens only when the gap between the two is very narrow and when one could perhaps with an effort achieve the same excellence as the other. As an amateur pianist, I might seek to emulate my next-door neighbour who is a little better pianist than I am, and I will very probably be jealous of him for that little extra proficiency. But I am not jealous of a Paderewski or Solomon, although they, too, are pianists. They are in no sense my rivals: they are my representatives. I think playing the piano is a fine thing, not because of what I do but because of what they do, or rather because of what I do through them. I myself may be a pretty poor hand at the art, but look what it becomes in *their* hands! And I, however humble, am of their company, and so I take pride in what they do because, look you, "we pianists" all belong together.

This principle of representation runs throughout the whole of human relations. The idea that service is degrading is an egalitarian superstition, for it is only in service that we really discover ourselves. And in serving our representative we are serving our best selves and we acquire a new dignity in the process. Notice how often Paul uses the word δοῦλος, a bondservant. Paul is the "bondservant" of Jesus Christ. Yet there is no servility in this, no sense of lowering the dignity of man, but rather an enhancement of it. These nonentities from the slums of Corinth and Rome and from the working class of the towns of Asia Minor were at one and the same time "bondservants" to Christ and "kings and priests unto God". The great paradox of Christianity is that "His service is perfect freedom", but the paradox was not invented by Christianity. There is always a tremendous sense of liberation to be found in service to the ideal, self counts for nothing and yet it counts for everything. It hands itself over to the beloved representative leader "just as thou wilt and when and where", but in so doing it knows itself a partaker of eternal life. This alone is life and victory. Nietzsche's idea that this is slave morality has a truth in it but not the truth that he intended.

> Make me a captive, Lord,
> And then I shall be free.
> Make me to render up my sword
> And I shall conqueror be.

In the Christian dispensation, therefore, the standards of moral conduct are to be found in the life and work of Christ and in loyalty to Him. They may look the same as the ethical virtues of unselfishness, helpfulness, speaking the truth, good temper, consideration, thrift, honesty, reliability, but they spring from a different root. In the beginning they can and ought to be "taught". If a child grows up in a household or a school in which these qualities are accepted they will become the things that are "done" and their opposites are "not done". The school, as we have seen, has a unique opportunity of making itself a community of this kind. Justice can be made to triumph in school even if it languishes in the world outside. Merit can find its reward, truth its appreciation, and mediocrity its true level. And this is done not by a display of texts but by the relations of the head to the staff and the staff to the pupils and the pupils to one another. In a world in which values have become so twisted that patriotism has become the last refuge of scoundrels it is throwing away an opportunity if we seek to make the school conform in every way to the world outside. John Dewey's theory to this effect can easily be overdone and made to issue in treating education as a kind of religious sanction—condoning if not justifying the state of society as it now is. To make the school an ideal society, however, is to provide the children with a standard by which they can challenge society outside and seek to reform it. They must therefore be helped to understand the existence of the moral principles on which their school community is based, and the spirit of that local community should both illustrate and justify those principles.

It is at the point of transfer from the smaller to the larger community outside that the peculiar nature of Christian ethics shows itself. How can a man be a Christian in the world of industry and business? Will the writing of "Honesty is the best Policy" at the age of ten save him? Will he fall into the heresy of believing that this adult world is the world of "reality" and that the idealism of his school community was a myth? Will he take refuge in the thought that the early Christians lived in little intimate communities far away and long ago and our world is utterly different from theirs? Will his religious education do no more for him than that? It has often been pointed out that the Quakers have been more successful than any other community in making this transfer from the idealism of the Quaker household to the rough and tumble of the world of business. Speaking truth and honest dealing had become so much second nature to them that their simple word was taken as sufficient security in the law courts and in the transactions of banking. If this has been so it is due to the fact that the Quaker meeting itself was a continuing society in which a man continued to live even while his affairs were also carried on in the same world of business occupied by the other people. The religious community and its standards were as "real" as the world outside. This surely is or ought to be the function of the Church in all denominations.

There is, however, a more ultimate necessity when the transfer has to be made from the sheltered life of home and school to the larger community. Moral maxims themselves have no power of inspiration apart from a context. They are simply words. The Christian community gives them a context, but the Christian community itself is dependent on something else. The term usually used of it is that it is the "body" of Christ, but by some strange perversion this term is commonly used to enhance the prestige of this or that denomination rather than as a challenge in the name of Christ to a human nature which needs re-making whether outside the Church or within it.

It is loyalty to Christ that is the real root of Christian ethics and at some point or other this and not merely the apprehension of moral principles at home or at school or even in the Church has to take its central place in the life of the Christian man. It is not a matter of what Christ did or what He said, actions or words to be slavishly and literally copied, but the forming of Christ within a man. Paul was very clear on this point. The many qualities of Christian love listed in I Corinthians xiii flow from Christ and are not independent of Him. And the virtues of love, joy, peace, long-suffering, kindness, goodness, faithfulness, meekness and temperance listed in Galatians v. 22, 23 are not temperamental but are the fruits of the Spirit and "against such there is no law". "And they that are of Christ Jesus have crucified the flesh with the passions and the lusts thereof". And finally, "if a man have not the *spirit* of Christ he is none of his". (Romans viii. 9.)

The character of Jesus is thus the standard of Christian morality. But we shall find that while the Bible makes this general rule quite clear it gives us only a limited number of illustrations. The Sermon on the Mount illustrates the Christian life in terms of the first century. What light does it throw on ethical problems in the twentieth? There is nothing about betting and gambling, white lies, Sunday games or cinemas, slavery or the credit system. Nevertheless, in the character of Jesus there is sufficient guidance even in these matters. We have to work out the details for ourselves. The primary concern of Jesus for persons rather than abstractions has already been mentioned. How far do football pools minister to the general good of all the persons taking part in them or of persons dependent upon the persons taking part in them? How do modern conditions affect the working-man's wife? Does her husband's forty-hour week lighten her own burden of household cares? Which person are we thinking of when we apply the personal standard to these problems? On the question of Sunday cinemas we may apply this personal standard, remembering the different kinds of persons to be benefited or burdened and the different ways of looking at the idea of "benefit". In this matter, however, there is a penetrating remark of Jesus Himself which is a rare enunciation of a principle, namely that "the Sabbath was made for man and not man for the Sabbath", and this is a text which may be given application to Sunday cinemas, golf, newspapers and football matches.

We may well be in the dark about the right thing to do, and good people may be divided in their position about them. What matters, however, is whether the right standard is being used. Of one thing we can be certain. The casuistical approach is quite at variance with New Testament attitude. Jesus (and Paul too) deals with questions as they arise and with the merits of the individual case, even though certain broad general principles stand out. But casuistry is an attempt to solve moral problems before they have arisen, on the assumption that when the situation does arise the factors will be those, and no more than those, which were considered in its theoretical presentation.

6

One characteristic of the mature mind as against the immature is the capacity both to take long views and to make them regulative of present conduct. It is here, too, where the distinction comes between primitive and civilized man and often also between the educated and the uneducated. The capacity to wait is one of those ethical virtues that indicate progress. It is, as we should expect, characteristic of Judaism and Christianity. "Wait thou upon God" is a continual refrain in the Old Testament. "Though the vision tarry, wait for it."[1] The same idea is found in the New Testament, where we are exhorted to watch as well as to pray. Bunyan's parable of the two children Passion and Patience is a variation on the same theme. Passion would have everything now, whereas Patience was content to wait for the suitable moment. The sentiment of loyalty is, as we have seen, capable of wide extension—from a particular person for a purely adventitious reason to a person of a more and more universal character. There is an extension in time as well as in content, and the training of a child in willingness to wait is in itself a preparation for greater moral qualities. Indeed it represents the prudential side of faith and is not to be confused either with indecision or with timidity.

It is doubtful whether a study of history has much effect as an education in moral conduct. The child who said that it was good for a King to learn what happened to King Charles I so that it might not happen to himself was expressing a point of view towards history very frequently held but for which evidence does not exist. History shows the consequences of actions but it provides scarcely at all either a stimulus or a deterrent for the future. It is the same argument that was used in favour of a savage penal code. It was argued that if potential wrongdoers knew that their acts would be severely punished they would refrain from doing them. This, of course, is allied to casuistry, for it treats an act in isolation from motive or

[1] Habakkuk ii. 3.

K

circumstance and provides a rigidly adjusted sequel for it. It ignores the emotional factors that are present in every situation and also the gambling instinct, which makes a man think that although it has never come off before, it might do so just this once! Moreover, the lesson of history is often that of success rather than of morality. It was Napoleon's success rather than his downfall that impressed Hitler, just as Julius Caesar was impressed by Alexander the Great. Besides, the fact that on the large scale of national history a king or a soldier or a politician has acted or suffered in a certain way is no particular guide to the plain man to go and do likewise except in those cases in which, as we have seen, the plain man can let himself be represented by the man who is a national figure.

7

In this discussion two factors intimately connected with standards have so far been omitted. It is now time to bring them in. One is conscience and the other discipline.

Standards are not always in themselves right or wrong; they may be merely convenient or preferable. But they all *feel* right or wrong and as such they are connected with conscience. Is conscience therefore a subject for religious education?

Conscience is often looked upon as a kind of litmus paper changing colour according to whether you are going right or wrong. Right is often defined as "that which conscience approves" and wrong as "that which conscience disapproves". This is really a circular definition, for "conscience" is then defined as something which "tells" us when we are doing right or wrong. It is usually added that doing right makes us feel happy and doing wrong makes us feel uncomfortable, and this is often the rough test which children are asked to apply. Conscience therefore would appear to be an emotion, and indeed the question whether or not this view is correct has been asked in a notable essay by Rashdall.[1] Unfortunately

[1] *Is Conscience an Emotion?*

the pleasure-pain principle works very loosely, for the feeling of discomfort gradually disappears if a man keeps on acting "against his conscience", and may even be rationalized away into duty or at any rate inevitability.

The idea of conscience as the categorical imperative is likewise faulty, yet to the individual that is what it is, and we do well to counsel children and indeed everybody to act according to their conscience. But that in itself does not prove that they are right, for people have made matters of conscience out of all sorts of strange things, such as working on Saturdays or vaccination against smallpox, which the majority of mankind would look upon as simply matters of opinion or evidence. In the case of pacifism equally convinced people can be found on both sides of the argument, each believing that it is the categorical imperative which has driven him into his position. A compelling principle which tells different people different things can be called a principle only in a very local sense.

Is conscience then simply something subjective? What is right for me is right, and I allow other people to differ from me. But this would be no principle at all, for the situation in which every man does what is right in his own eyes is clearly one of anarchy and irresponsibility. Personal preference and expediency cannot be exalted into those moral principles to deny which a man is denying himself.

Is it then, as Trotter's notable book would have it,[1] something which is the product of society? The conventional thing to do is that which society approves and to act according to the *mores* of the group is to act according to your conscience, while acting against them produces that sense of outlawry which is a marked feature everywhere of acting against conscience. But this again does not get us very far. Men have been found conscientiously to act *against* the *mores* of their community, and we have to ask ourselves whence came the motive which made them do it? Mere conventionality can be set aside by a higher expediency and in that case no principle

[1] *Instincts of the Herd in Peace and War*, by W. Trotter.

is involved. But the instinct of the herd may act as a plus or
as a minus. It may be suggestible or it may be contra-suggest-
ible. In some cases *Athanasius contra mundum* is a psychological
condition and not at all a moral attitude.

What then is conscience and how can it be educated?

There are two factors in conscience—a constant and a
contingent. The constant is the innate sense of right and
wrong possessed by everyone. It is a power of polarizing
experience to the north or south poles of a moral standard.
But what *specific* things are right or wrong depends upon
society. If I am a conscientious objector to vaccination I must
follow my conscience, and if it is the law of the land that I
must be vaccinated against smallpox I have broken the law
and must put up with the consequences. But my willingness
to endure suffering does not prove that my conscience was
right. All it proves is that I am a sincere and honest, if
misguided, man. My conscience needs educating, and it is
part of the work of religious education to educate people's
consciences. How is it done?

We begin with this constant factor and try to establish
the habit of children acting by their conscience. This indeed
is radical, for to treat a sense of right or wrong as if it were
no more than a matter of opinion or a sense of discomfort is
to make moral action impossible. The thing that is considered
to be right may appear to us perhaps to be a triviality, but the
task is to educate the conscience rather than to suggest that
it be ignored. A sense of moral values, however arrived at,
is a rock upon which character can be built, whereas a general
sense that one thing is as good as another and that nothing
really *matters* is the quicksand which has swallowed up many
an imposing structure.

Conscience, however, in the very young is equated with
the habits of the family. "Right" is "what we do at our
house", and any difference from it is wrong. When the
habits of our house conflict with those of other houses, as we
soon discover at school, we cannot easily keep up the position
that only we are right just because it is what the family does.

Some new ground has to be found for the old belief, or the belief or practice has to give place to one which is accepted by a wider group than our own family. This problem often causes genuine agony to quite small children without their realizing what all the trouble is about. It was an article of belief in my own nursery days that Santa Claus came down the chimney. At school, however, it turned out that Santa Claus was your own father and mother. The shock of this conflict was no less severe than the later shock in finding that Isaiah did not write all the book attributed to him. The gallant fight for orthodoxy ended, however, in the sorrowful elimination of Santa Claus.

School, then, takes the place of the family. The small group gives way to the larger, but still conscience is chiefly concerned with custom. At my school it was held by all the families concerned that it was wrong to play tennis on Sundays. This family view had been strengthened by corroboration. But at college it was no longer a matter of "wrong" any more than playing tennis was "right". It did not appear to be a matter of conscience at all. And while the conflict of conscience with conscience may be very stimulating, even if exhausting, the conflict of conscience with indifference is the nearest equivalent in the spiritual world to shadow boxing. There is no opponent to hit. Nevertheless it helps to educate the conscience, for it has to give a reason for existence *in itself* and not in contrast to some opposition.

And so we go on, constantly coming up against unfamiliar matters of conscience and perhaps equally unfamiliar matters of indifference, and the conscience becomes educated by having to meet the challenge of an ever-widening circle of loyalties. The result of this is the gradual but fundamental discovery that a great number of our attitudes are no more than opinions, preferences, habits and matters of convenience, and that there are very very few to deny which would be to deny ourselves and to sink in the scale of our own self-respect. In the long run that is what conscience really is—that standard which we accept as being our true intrinsic selves, and to fall below which would be a negation of life itself. It is not a matter of willingness to suffer, for men have suffered for all kinds of strange causes. It is a matter of ultimate valuation in the sight of God, and although some men have arrived even at this highest level with very bizarre accoutrements, it was their education that was at fault and not their moral character.

The education of conscience, therefore, is of the highest importance in religious education. And it is here where the greatest danger lies for the teacher. To train children, for example, in the belief that to attend a council school is to do despite to Almighty God, maker of heaven and earth, is to exalt a mere matter of opinion or convenience into a principle that divides light from dark, heaven from hell. This sort of irresponsible playing with eternal verities as counters in the denominational game is the real blasphemy against the Holy Spirit. Religious education can be the most far-reaching form of education and needs to be entered upon with a due sense of responsibility. The education of conscience does not mean bringing up children to agree with you and putting the fear of God into them if they do not. It means introducing them to continually wider spheres of interest, helping them gradually to exclude all matters of pure expediency from the region of absolute values, honouring them for acting by their conscience at whatever stage it has arrived, and so coming to see all time and all existence in the light of the knowledge of God. And then the further discovery will be made that conscience can be educated by deeper insight as well as by wider knowledge, for there is a ''beyond that is also within''.

8

I have already used the simile of the marsh and the stream. They may contain the same amount of water but the second is usable and the first is not.

So is it with the human spirit. Men's minds are a hotchpotch of ideas unorganized, impulses uncontrolled and ideals unfulfilled. The purpose of discipline is to make them usable. The co-ordinated mind and integrated spirit are products of the right kind of education and in the eyes of many people they are quite impossible to achieve without religion. For they are produced ideally by loyalty and the quality of that loyalty determines the nature of that integration. To Paul it was the life in Christ that unified his own life and gave it coherence and purpose.

The word "discipline" itself implies this. Discipline is the art of being a disciple, of accepting authority, of following a leader. There are therefore two sides to it—that of the pupil and that of the teacher. If the children are to be disciples, are you worthy to be a leader? If it be said that they are to become disciples not of the teacher but of Christ, how can that happen except the teacher himself is a disciple worthy of imitation? "Be ye imitators of me," says Paul to the Corinthians, "as I am of Christ." Discipline is a matter of example more than of precept. The leader, as we have seen, incarnates in himself that which the follower most desires and wants to be. He is the person who does best what all his followers do well. And he himself is a follower.

The experience of being a member of the Oxford Bach Choir in the days of Professor Sir Hugh Allen was very enlightening in the matter of discipline. Allen used to storm at us, bully us, work us hard, trample on our feelings and do everything which from an outsider's view would put us off. But we were not put off, we enjoyed it. And for two reasons. First, we earnestly wanted to do it properly and we knew that he knew just *how* it ought to be done. Secondly, he himself was body, mind and spirit under authority also—the authority of Johann Sebastian Bach. If he bullied us he bullied himself still more. If he would not let us escape with the second best, however good it was, we knew that he would accept no second-rate standard for himself either. His authority was not giving orders but being himself the perfect disciple, and to serve him was that service which is perfect freedom.

Are there, however, no day-to-day methods that can be followed to help children to discover this self-discipline? Children easily follow a leader, but the habit quite often ends in itself and they take no responsibility for themselves. Four very practical hints can be offered.

First, the habit of decision. We grow morally by making decisions, even decisions as simple as that between tea and coffee at breakfast-time. To say "I don't mind which" may be true but precisely because it is true a decision has to be made. There is no particular morality in continuing to follow a strong preference, for the choice in that case has been predetermined. But to make up your mind in matters where the choice is genuine, and to stand by your decision is the line of growth. To keep the mind continually open, or continually to reopen questions which have already been decided, not because new light has come but in order to preserve one's "freedom", is corrosive of the human spirit and is a sure road to anarchy. Broadmindedness is the product of conviction and is as far removed from indifference as it is from bigotry.

Secondly, we may copy the excellent practice of Rowland Hill and give "no credit for bits". Tasks have got to be carried through to the end. An approximation where exactitude is possible is culpable negligence and deserves no consideration. A good deal of modern education fails just at this point. It is so much concerned with preventing the child being bored that it deprives him of the satisfaction of seeing a job well done, finished off, packed up and labelled for export! It requires not only great strength of mind on the part of the teacher to see that this is done, but also the power of inspiring faith that the thing is really worth doing and that there will be a thrill at the end of it. All education involves a gradual substitution of long views for short views, and to be content with immediate results which can earn no greater praise than "It will do" is a regression into an earlier state of childhood. And this is true in matters of the spirit. If a standard is capable of being reached it must be reached.

There is value, therefore, in not pitching our ideals too high and disheartening our pupils with impossible tasks. At the same time they need to be such to call out that effort and enthusiasm which can survive a long intermediate period of drudgery.

A third practical hint is to accustom children to a right use of discretion. "A Brownie," it is said, "gives in to others: she never gives in to herself." At what point, however, does this change-over occur? It is clearly wrong to give in to other people all the time. Indeed the very phrase "give in" conveys an unfortunate suggestion: "takes consideration for" would be much better. Discrimination in sorting out those matters which are of trivial importance and those for which one ought to make a stand is very good moral training. It helps to give perspective and by getting one into the habit of weighing issues before one decides whether to fight or to ignore them relieves a situation of just that measure of emotional quality which might result both in hasty action and in subsequent remorse.

Fourthly, one goal of all religious education should be good manners. I have already indicated that the roots of good manners are in natural religion, but they can come to fruition in Christianity. Unfortunately they often wither and die in this ampler air. Men are to be found who in the general relationships of life are considerate and tactful, anticipating requests for services which they can render, courteous in speech and gesture, and yet in argument will abuse their opponents and throw about such words as "reactionary", "heretic", "schismatic" and "liberal". To be able to distinguish between a man and his opinions is an art almost entirely lost over the greater part of the earth's surface today. As we have seen, good manners are a product of humility, and in the Christian scheme of things humility is a by-product of a man's saving knowledge of God. Good manners are sacramental. They are an outward and visible sign of an inward and spiritual grace. More than that, they help to produce and intensify that grace which gave them birth, and they are far more relevant to the fruits of the spirit than is any mere orthodoxy of doctrine. There are those who say "Lord, Lord" who are nevertheless stigmatized in the saying of Jesus as unprofitable servants.

Discipline, therefore, is a method of achieving desired ends. Men discipline themselves in diet and sleep when training for the boat race. The pianist keeps up his skill by the discipline of continual practice. If the end is really ardently desired, discipline is not difficult. It mostly depends on how ardently you desire it. Robert Lynd, speaking of his school-days, once said, "Short of work there wasn't anything I wouldn't do to become a Greek scholar". And short of work there isn't anything most people wouldn't do in order to become a good Christian. But it is in that idea "short of work" that there is the rub.

CHAPTER VIII

DOCTRINE

I

IT is symptomatic of the intellectualizing of the Christian faith that to nearly everybody the term "orthodoxy" suggests only its original meaning of "correct" doctrine rather than good manners. The goal of Christian education is thus supposed to be the acceptance of orthodoxy. This kind of thing is exactly paralleled in Communism, where correctness of doctrine is esteemed above those qualities that make for decent living. It is not always realized that this is an illustration of the old "transfer of training" fallacy, for there is no transfer from the acceptance of a scheme of ideas to the power to live a better life. But it is only too often the case that this does not matter, for ideas rather than better living are the desired end and there is nothing sought beyond them.

The position given to doctrine in religious education depends therefore upon your conception of truth. Is truth something propositional, a matter of words and ideas, or is it something organic and expressed in persons rather than words? "Ye shall know the truth," says the New Testament, "and the truth shall make you free." Does this mean that you know that Jesus was the second person of the Trinity, that He rose from the dead, and that the true Church has descended from the Apostles by continuous ordination—and that having got to know these things you are then free? If so, we must then ask, free from what? A previous generation would have said free from hell, and the Athanasian Creed makes clear that that is so. But how is it so? Does it mean that if you do not believe what the bishop or your Sunday school teacher tells you God is prepared to blast your whole existence for evermore? We are all too ready to identify our own self-will with the eternal purposes of God, as if this identification cleared us at once of all charges of egotism.

So inveterate are our intellectual habits once they have been acquired that we nearly always associate meaning with thinking rather than with feeling. Accordingly, in church membership, when taken seriously, a very large part is played by belief and the sooner belief is formulated the better it is held to be for the person concerned. The catechism makes its appearance at an early age in church schools, in other Sunday schools there is the memorizing of "golden texts" and "portions" of Scripture, while the amount of dogma that the Catholic child is believed to be capable of absorbing is quite astonishing. We have seen that there are good psychological grounds in favour of this practice, for learning by heart comes easily to children and by continual repetition doctrine becomes an early and permanent possession which can wait for later years for its interpretation. The "religions of authority" have the advantage here over the "religions of the spirit", for they are not self-conscious about their propaganda and do not in the least mind providing children with knowledge beyond their years. This creates in the minds of some people an almost superstitious attachment to doctrine, so that they feel all the emotions of fear and anger if afterwards they hear it challenged.

Yet while this familiarizing of the child with doctrine has a great deal to do with church membership, it has nothing necessarily to do with religion. It is possible to be a fiercely loyal Anglican or Catholic or Nonconformist without being a religious person at all. As we have already seen, it is one of the commonest fallacies in religious education that knowledge of words produces a change of heart.

Nevertheless words in some contexts acquire a power which they do not in themselves possess. Statements of faith are to be found not only in catechisms but also in liturgies, and this association with worship gives them an emotional tinge which helps to make the idea behind them more easily assimilated. On this side of religious education the Free Churches of England are seriously handicapped by the omission of articles of faith in the ordinary ritual of service, although it may be urged that their theology is found in their hymns. Moreover, although they are, so to speak, "based on the Bible", it is probable that the average church-going Anglican hears more of the Bible read in a twelve-month (even excluding the Psalms) than does the average church-going Nonconformist. The liturgy of the Church can be a very effective agency of religious education.

Doctrine, moreover, need not be the dead thing that it so often is. The real test of the validity of a doctrine is not whether it was or was not carried by a majority vote at Nicaea or Trent or Westminster but whether it is or is not capable of re-creating the experience out of which it arose. A good deal of doctrine is no doubt as purely speculative as the Hindu doctrine of *Karma*, a kind of ecclesiastical mathematics true within its own limited universe of discourse but meaning nothing outside it. It is none the less interesting, of course, and it is as intellectually stimulating as a cross-word puzzle, but like a cross-word puzzle the words are present in isolation.

On the other hand there are other doctrines, as, for example, the eternal sonship of Christ, or imputed righteousness, or the communion of saints, to the understanding of which even the adolescent can bring something from his own experience of life. They "speak to our condition", but the complicated language in which they have come down to us is due to the attempt to express in one medium something which is experienced in another. Paul not only had to borrow terms from other religions and give them new meaning, but also had to invent terms of his own. But the analysis of Christian experience into regeneration, justification, sanctification, adoption and the other Pauline categories does not deny the reality of the experience itself, and when the experience of God is present this way of thinking about it helps to keep it alive and deepen it. The misuse of doctrine comes when it is used as the *initial* qualification for membership instead of being the final expression of that spiritual achievement which it is the function of membership to make possible. Nothing is more unedifying than to hear essentially worldly-minded men using doctrine in this way. Those who are glib with words will always be able to appear more "orthodox" than those who have the reality of the experience but find words to be a difficulty. Nevertheless, there are undoubtedly some to whom the intellectual grasp of doctrine is in itself a genuine way of experiencing God.

2

In order to neutralize the pseudo-reverential atmosphere that envelops all matters of doctrine it is well that the teacher should be clear from the start that every doctrine of whatever kind is man-made. This applies alike to the doctrine of the Trinity, the doctrine of the dictatorship of the proletariat, or the doctrine of the survival of the fittest. That a doctrine concerns what are called "holy things" does not eliminate this cardinal fact. Although it is the view, for instance, of certain groups that the doctrine of the Trinity was "revealed" by God (presumably because no normally constituted persons could possibly have invented it), we can nevertheless trace its origin and progress in the discussions of theologians. To consider doctrines as sacrosanct is to pay too great a compliment to the committees that formulated them. When Paul spoke of a man's life being "hid with Christ in God" he was saying something utterly different from "believing that God is one". The devils also believe, says the Epistle of James.

What then was he saying? For it is with Paul that Christian doctrine is supposed to have arisen. It has already been indicated that it is a mistake to think of him expounding a body of doctrine called Paulinism. Rather he was seeking to put into words his experience of Christ. Like

all men who have to wrestle with overwhelming experiences
he found that words were at best but poor approximations.
Consequently he is obscure in many places and appears to be
using words without any regard to their ordinary meaning.
If Peter on the mount of transfiguration "wist not what to
answer" and so talked nonsense (Mark ix. 5-6) it was
not unlikely that Paul "caught up to the third heaven"
(II Corinthians xii. 2) should have experiences which also
paralysed both speech and writing. Take, for instance, this
great text: "We all, with unveiled face reflecting as a mirror
the glory of the Lord, are transformed into the same
image from glory to glory, even as from the Lord the Spirit"
(II Corinthians iii. 18). That, I maintain, is poetry and it completely loses its point when taken to pieces and expounded
bit by bit. By similar treatment Keats' *Ode to the Nightingale*
and a fugue of Bach would also lose their point. To give
exactitude to the phrases "from glory to glory" or to load
the word "transformed" with doctrinal significance is to
ignore the Pauline injunction that spiritual things are discerned spiritually and is to be untrue to the spirit of Paul
himself. Consistency in language is not his strong point and he
uses "the spirit of God" and the "spirit of Christ" inter-
changeably. But what does it matter? "Religious definitions
are always attempts at salvage, but Paul had not suffered
shipwreck over the problem of Christ's person."[1]

If then we begin with Paul we begin with him certainly
not as a doctrinaire theologian. His epistles were almost
always *ad hoc*, dealing with practical problems in a practical
way, and were so far from being treatises that the Epistle
to the Romans, for instance, has no less than four separate
endings—three separate postscripts. Nevertheless Paul indicates the true nature of doctrine. It is an attempt at the
verbal expression of a spiritual experience, and it is concerned
not so much with exact words as with exact categories.

Indeed, the more exact the words the more the categories
are misunderstood. The painful striving of the Athanasian

[1] Deissmann, *Paul: a Study in Social and Religious History*, p. 143.

Creed after exact expression leaves the reader with the irritating sense that the Trinity has more to do with logic than it has with God.   On the other hand any sympathetic reader of Paul's writings realizes that the term Trinity was coined later to indicate that there is one God, who upholds the universe, and that the Jesus of history and the Spirit of Christ, the Holy Spirit, the Spirit of God (whichever name you choose is, according to Paul, quite matterless) do not stand over against Him but are to be identified only in connection with Him.   It is that category of Being which it is important to grasp rather than any exact terminology.   Exactness of terminology, however, has had this great attraction for the natural man who lies embedded in all Christians in that it provides a quick and easy way of unchurching the folk with whom you disagree.   And Church history is disfigured by this kind of process which is quite alien to Paul's own thought.   "In every way, whether in pretence or in truth, Christ is proclaimed; and therein I rejoice, yea, and will rejoice". (Philippians i. 18.)

The difficulty, however, with theological categories is that they are apt to be drawn from our own experience but in reverse.   We say, for instance, that God is sovereign, omnipotent, omniscient and omnipresent—ideas which are either completely meaningless or, if they mean anything, deprive God of any personal character whatever.   These ideas are drawn from our own experience rather than from an understanding of what Jesus showed God to be.   We cannot do everything: God can.   We do not know everything: God does. We cannot be everywhere: God is everywhere.   We cannot overrule the statecraft of this world: God can.   In other words you take the list of the disabilities of human nature, turn them round, and there you have the character of God.   Nothing shows so clearly the man-made nature of doctrine as this. Granted that if we must use words to describe the attributes of God we can but use the categories that we ourselves know.   This is true.   But there is a wise anthropomorphism as well as an unwise, and this reversal of human attributes is just as unwise as its opposite in Greek mythology, where gods were really men, with passions just like ours.

These categories of power, knowledge and existence are not the only categories concerned in human life. There are others which offer no such easy definition, namely faith, hope and love, and when we move into realms such as these we notice that these are categories not of precision but of value and that they are apprehended not as a mathematical formula but as beauty is apprehended. Who can say what constitutes a beautiful scene or picture or melody? To attempt to do so in words is by that very act to move outside the orbit of the thing that you are trying to describe. Religious experience is fundamentally an æsthetic experience rather than an intellectual exercise. Like all æsthetic experiences it is capable of infinite analysis even though it cannot be synthesized, for it is born whole. All the mighty mass of *Shakespeareana*, the centuries of criticism and exposition and explanation, could not have created one Shakespeare play. And in the same way the endless mass of theological speculation, definition and criticism could none of it act as a substitute for the living Christ in the soul of man.

We must constantly be on our guard against any attempted substitution. Nothing is more flattering to human nature than to feel that you have captured the eternal God within your own thought forms and that you know all the answers. In education this results in formalism, for formalism means giving the answers without showing the working, and sometimes without being able to show it. Its aim, therefore, is acceptance, conformity, obedience, and its method is propaganda.

So far with the difficulties. But there is a positive side of doctrine which avoids them. If doctrine is really the expression—or the attempted expression—of experience, its truth can be ascertained from its ability to play back that experience. And for this the formalism of a creed offers very little opportunity. Indeed a creed is not strictly doctrine at all—

L

it is a table of contents of the faith, and it is called in Greek a "symbol", i.e. originally a tally, or identity card. But the kind of doctrine that has proved to be the most able to be re-transformed into experience is that found in poetry. In the Christian Church the Psalms have been genuine repositories of doctrine, and it is in Christian hymnology that the closest approximation has been reached to an understanding of the faith. It was with wise insight that John Wesley called his first hymn book "a body of experience and practical divinity". The hymns have crystallized experience in suggestive words far more effectively than any doctrinal statement that was ever penned at Chalcedon or Augsburg or Lambeth, and they have afforded a rapid re-translation into experience. By metaphor, suggestion and rhythm it is possible to convey exactly that which a plain statement must always convey inexactly. There is the same whole world of difference between *Rock of Ages* and the Thirty-nine Articles as there is between Shakespeare's *Julius Caesar* and a catalogue of *Shakespeareana*. Poetry always has this advantage over prose—it can suggest whereas prose can only state; and you can suggest wholeness but you can never state it.

3

There is a further characteristic of doctrine. It is not only man-made (none the worse for that, of course, for how could it be otherwise?) but also it is developed by contrast, opposition, over-emphasis and by the influence of circumstances. To take the last first, it is clear from the Pauline epistle that the Jewish law, the whole mechanism of slavery and manumission and the practice of the Roman law courts provided the handiest illustrations when Paul came to write about what Christ had done for him. Those terms which to us appear as abstract nouns were to his first hearers most vivid metaphors. Similarly the social structure of feudalism is at the back of Anselm's doctrine of the atonement. German pietism of the seventeenth century took its colour from the need to escape the horrors of the Thirty Years War and the Barthian doctrine of the sovereignty of God is the cry of the politically helpless Christian in the throes of the Nazi persecution. The present fashion for the theology of Kierkegaard is significant of the sense of frustration that there is in the modern world. This social and political background of doctrine is a most interesting study and it prevents the mood of the moment from being taken too seriously. It is, of course, not the whole story. It gives only the form in which some vital aspect of Christian faith clothes itself for the time being.

The development of doctrine by opposition has a very important consequence for religious education. Schools of theological thought succeed one another, and if one were to abstract from almost any book of theology those sections in which the author is criticizing his predecessors, there would often be very little left. It is here where there is often a false analogy drawn between progress in theology and progress in science. The scientist carries on his researches and each step in progress outmodes what has gone before. His successor starts where the previous man left off and science text-books are out of date and useless almost within a decade of their publication. The reason is not that the earlier scientists were "wrong" and that the later ones have "refuted" them, but that all scientists being in continual and vital contact with their raw material, the phenomena of the universe, have their own first-hand reference to original sources. Beginning where his successor left off, the next man, with that advantage, makes new discoveries regarding the raw material common to them all.

Now progress in theology *looks* as if it were the same but it is quite different. And that for two reasons.

First, every sincere expression of religious experience represents something that is eternally true in the relations of God with man. It is the fashion today among certain rather younger theologians to pour scorn on what they call "liberalism". As we have already noticed (page 63)

one book in particular is designated for the scrap-heap—
T. R. Glover's *The Jesus of History* (1917). The idea is that we
have now advanced far beyond it just as we have gone still
farther away from Ritschl and Schleiermacher (though not
apparently from Calvin or Aquinas!). But if, as has been said,
progress in religion is likened not to a march along a road
but to the growing of a tree, there are certain rings of growth
which have to be made and when made become an integral
part of the tree. The so-called "liberal" school is one of them.
It corresponds to a stage in Christian experience which cannot
be left out. Consequently at a certain period of adolescence
(and in the Christian life adolescence is not confined to the
years 14 to 25 but may be found equally at 50 or 70) the one
really important book to give to an enquirer is Glover's
Jesus of History. What he says there is eternally true, and the
fact that it is not the whole truth does not take away from the
value of what truth there is. At this stage the chief doctrinal—
if it be doctrinal—need is the assurance that Jesus Christ
really lived, that He was not a myth created by the later
Church, and that the word "Christ" represents more than a
theological lay figure. If Christianity is a historical religion
this historical reference is, always has been and always will
be fundamental.

The second reason is that while science must be constantly
in contact with its raw material and its truth is tested by that
contact theology is continually slipping away from its first
reference. Theologians can and do criticize theologians
without any reference whatever to the "raw material"
with which they are all concerned—i.e. ordinary folks,
and their relation to the God who made them. The result
can be seen in the theological colleges. In some of them
what Dr. James Denny (no mean scholar) called "the superstition of Hebrew and Greek" has still first and not
second place, and in some it is considered more repre-
hensible for a man to leave without an adequate knowledge
of "Proctor and Frere" or of Wesley's Forty-Four Sermons
than without any knowledge at all of the personal, sexual,

social and religious needs of their own fellow-countrymen. These ought they to have done and not left the other undone. It is not surprising that to intelligent but not always informed outsiders doctrine is so much word-spinning and those who insist upon it are like those who

> Grate on their scrannel pipes of wretched straw:
> The hungry sheep look up, and are not fed.

Doctrine, therefore, has to be treated "educationally". We are thinking beings and we must needs express our experiences in thoughts and the thoughts in words. It is also a necessity to be as exact as possible in the framing of these words, always remembering the different meanings of "exactness" as in prose and poetry. Loose thinking, the use of shibboleths, half-truths and that parade of curious information which is the veneer of ignorance are an insult to human intelligence and work not to the glory of God. The fact that doctrine will not take us the whole way is no justification for not going with it as far as we can. But to use it as a substitute for Christian living, to exalt logical orthodoxy over against love and justice, to count obedience to authority superior to the plain movings of conscience is to fall into idolatry, substituting the name of the thing for the thing itself.

It is well, therefore, to see where doctrine came from in the first instance, to see the background, for example, of the great Chalcedonian definition, to see *why* the doctrine of the Trinity had to be formulated, to recover the feeling of those years when Luther was preaching justification by faith as a counterblast to justification by works, and to try to understand how it was possible in the present atomic age for an Italian Pope to promulgate the new dogma of the bodily assumption of the Virgin Mary. The *ecology* of doctrine is a very fruitful study and every teacher of religion needs to pursue it. It represents the historical method applied to the New Testament, the Creeds and the Councils. This is one meaning of the term "studying doctrine educationally".

Another meaning is that the subject must be graded.

With young children doctrine comes in not at all as such. It is accepted that Jesus is "Son of God", that He rose from the dead, that the Bible is "the Word of God". These and other doctrines are taken for granted and for children are expressed best in hymns. The theology of the hymn "There is a green hill far away" may be somewhat old-fashioned, but it is adequate when it comes to young children. At a later stage, when children are more concerned with action than with stories, the *principle* behind the Boy Scout's good deed for the day will be a very useful approach to the Christian faith. When, later still, the time arrives that a young person or a Christian enquirer begins to be concerned with problems concerning God and Christ we need to be clear in our own minds concerning aims and procedure. Here we must keep a firm hold upon history and not allow ourselves to be misled by abstractions. The sense of God "in the starry sky above and the moral law within" will be intuitively present in the children already and the "informing" of this sense needs to begin with doctrine not of God but of Christ. The Ritschlian approach will probably be found to be the most useful. God is like Christ and Christ has to us the value of God. Christ is the leader who exemplifies obedience to the highest moral law, and was the first in a great historical succession. The Christian life begins and rises to perfection through the historic community of believers within which the work of Christ is continued into every generation. If the historical view of the Bible is to be accepted and to condition our interpretation of Christianity, it is inevitable that the doctrinal setting will be of this nature. It is not a permanent stage, of course, but neither is childhood a permanent stage, and Lowell's hackneyed lines are vitally true in matters of religious education:

> God sends His teachers into every age
> With revelation suited to their growth.

There is far too much intimidation by theologians or by would-be theologians over the souls and consciences of those who are beginning the Christian life. The latest view is not always the best, and even if it is, it is not necessarily the best for every person at any given moment.

God then is like Christ, and this is a much more *educational* approach to doctrine than the other way round. At any rate we do know something—the nature and the work of our Lord. There is here a foundation on which to build. To declare at too early a stage that Christ is like God is to compel us to answer first What is God like *apart* from Christ? and circular reasoning is only too easy. The great value of stating the doctrine the other way round is that it gives us a standard which we can at once apply to the Bible. The problem of the drowning of Pharaoh, the slaughter of the Amalekites, the imprecatory psalms, are clearly not up to this standard at all and the child can make his own historical criticism of the Bible without feeling that he must give it up altogether. Here is the foundation of a reasonable doctrine of inspiration arising not from "higher critical" views but from the plain fact that many things in the Bible are not up to the required level.

4

The question of teaching doctrine *as such* clearly does not arise till later and even then it is wise to keep it closely connected with both history and experience. It can so easily become a separate "subject" altogether, completely divorced even from religion. The saints have seen this all down the ages no matter what the theologians have said. "Of what doth it profit," says Thomas à Kempis, "if thou art able to discourse learnedly concerning the Trinity and lack compassion, and so art displeasing to the Trinity?"

Nowhere is this more true than in the Christian doctrine of man. That Christ died for our sins is true, but *how* is it true? What is the meaning of sin, and how can a fact in time such as the Crucifixion have any effect upon my own wrong-doing two millenia after the event? These are theological questions, but the value of discussing them is almost lost unless the teacher can see them in terms of living men and living problems. This is not to equate the power and purpose of God with complete exactness to present needs. He still remains beyond all that we can ask or think. He is still, as von Hügel loved to say, a "vast surplusage". But the appreciation of that fact is gradually realized as we go along. It too is an intense experience of the soul and not a dogma accepted on authority. Where we begin, however, is where we are, and that place is marked by the plain needs of man for a God who is as Christ showed him to be. Any theological speculation which leaves this out of account is irrelevant at this point. And the temper of this age is such that men are unaware of their own deepest needs. A Christian doctrine of man must surely begin with that diagnosis.

It is in later adolescence that this becomes urgent, for at this stage self-consciousness is marked by doubt and questioning if not by unrest. At a low level of understanding there is a desire for the slick short answer, a habit which the intellectualizing of our time encourages. For such minds there are plenty of books available, particularly on the Catholic side. This, however, like all intellectualism, is a form of escapism. Micah asks, "Shall I give the fruit of my body for the sin of my soul?" and the parallel question, "Shall I give the findings of my intellect for the sin of my soul?" is not inappropriate. If, however, we feel that modern psychology has something to say at this point we shall discover that Susan Isaacs' three needs of men—for security, for affection and for significance—are translatable into theological terms. It is from this angle that we may now consider the place of doctrine in religious education.

5

(a) Security is of many kinds. We obviously need physical, social and political security. But we also need security one towards another. The child or the adult needs security in his relations with his teacher. He needs to know just where he stands, and consistency of treatment is a fundamental requirement. This can perfectly well co-exist with correction, admonition, criticism and difference of opinion. But it involves complete confidence in the teacher's probity and concern for his pupils' welfare. There is nothing more disintegrating for a person—or for a dog—than uncertainty in the relations he has with people with whom he is vitally concerned. To be stroked and cajoled at one moment and the next to be stormed at or slighted destroys self-confidence and warps character. And it is one of the cardinal tenets of the Christian faith that this consistency is to be found in God. It took Israel a long time to discover this fact, although it is implicit in the psalms. God is unchangeable not only in His essence but also in His character. In the heights of our enthusiasm He is with us, and "though we make our bed in Sheol" He is there also. He is concerned for his children like a father; even when our sins come between us and Him His character is unchanged. And the New Testament presses this truth home still more. What is the "forgiveness" of God if it is not the mark of His unchanging love? With Him we know where we are. There is security in that thought. He is the rock on which we build, the tower into which we flee, His righteousness is like the strong mountains, His judgements are a great deep, He is from everlasting to everlasting, God for ever and ever. This is not the language of an abstract dogmatism, it is the teaching of Christ and it is the heartfelt experience of Christian men.

This sense of security is important in adolescence because of the concern that there is with time and space. The vastness of the universe brings to some men what Dr. H. G. Wood has called "astronomical intimidation" and they never grow out of it. The universe is like a great Juggernaut-car riding ruthlessly on its way over the insignificant bodies of men. Moreover, the belief that it has been doing this sort of thing for millions of years still further emphasizes that insignificance. It is therefore important to realize that the

determining of these distances of time and space has been
the deposit of men's thinking, and that other men have also
affirmed that although this universe may have the appearance
of a vast self-acting machine it has a driver, and the driver's
concern is to keep out of the way of men instead of destroying
them.   He created them in the first instance and so why
should he wantonly destroy his own creation?   Again this
is the plain teaching of Jesus. Not a sparrow falls to the ground
without our Father being concerned about it, and men are of
more account than sparrows.   And from the beginning of
time, before the mountains were brought forth or ever He had
formed the earth and the world He has been what we know
Him from the New Testament to be.   The "friend behind
phenomena", as Dr. Gilbert Murray speaks of Him, is the
God of love. We know His name and His nature. He is
our Father and the whole universe is but our Father's house.

(b) The need for affection shows itself at various levels.
Whether "everybody's loved by someone" or not, everybody
wishes to be loved and to love. This may be no more than the
desire for an emotional companionship not concerned with
any one person in particular and not necessarily permanent,
but even at this level it is nevertheless the yearning of the
heart for completeness, since no person is or can be complete
in himself. The fact that we are spiritual beings as well as
bodies and minds means that we require satisfaction on the
spiritual plane as well as in other ways. The love of one person
for another is just such a satisfaction and is, so to speak, an
experience in the fourth dimension. And the deeper the level
we reach in this relationship the greater is its spiritual content
and the more we come to an understanding of the deepest
level of all, the relation of the soul to God. For all experiences of love belong to the same universe of discourse, and if
our hearts find no rest it is because they cannot be completely
satisfied with anything less than rest in God.

But there are unsuspected factors in these experiences.
The first is that they have a physical side to them and the
physical is sacramental to the spiritual. The appreciation,

moreover, of love on the physical side is of the same quality as the appreciation of physical beauty. In both cases we have to stand in a certain austere aloofness from the object of appreciation because any thought of possessiveness ruins the relationship. This is the theme of one of the stories in George Macdonald's *Phantastes* and is the motif of the Greek folk-tale of Daphne, the nymph who was changed into a tree when her lover tried to grasp her. Yet it is this austerity which gives not only greater permanence to the relationship but also greater enjoyment, just as it is possessiveness that turns it all to ashes and corrupts the very good within us into evil. The astringent element in the love relationship lies in the fact that for either person to use the other as an object makes it for ever impossible. If this experience at its best transcends those of everyday existence, the introduction into it of sordid considerations removes it at once from the spiritual realm where it is intended to be and reduces it to earthiness.

Nevertheless two persons are concerned and not one. The perfection of the relationship has an ambivalent result, for at one and the same time there is a keen sense of unity and also an enhanced sense of difference. It is in the austere and yet enthusiastic giving of oneself and the willingness to be as nothing for the sake of the other person that one really finds one's own individuality. The danger of slipping over from these heights into the abyss of self-justification at the other's expense is always present. There is a by-way to hell, according to Bunyan, even at the very gate of the Celestial City. We are playing with fire all the time, for we are mortal beings experiencing something which, however momentary, is beyond mortality. Primitive man with a sure instinct saw there was danger in every such situation, and the system of taboo came into existence to lay down the safety rules. The tension consists in these two contraries, individuality and union, being each fully experienced at one and the same time.

Lest this should seem a long way from the question of the teaching of doctrine let us recall the fact that doctrine to be sound always represents experience somewhere. Doctrine concerning the soul's relationship to God in love cannot but have reference to all personal relations in which love is the link. While in theory the Divine is so far transcendent that our relations with Him must be altogether different from those among ourselves, in actual matter-of-fact experience it is not entirely so. Love to our brother whom we have seen is connected with love to God whom we have not seen, and in the first Epistle of John the second is made to depend upon the first. All that I have said hitherto about love and beauty has its parallel in Christian experience and can therefore be expressed in doctrinal terms. And if we do not begin here, where can we begin?—only with some *a priori* theory about God which there is no means of verifying. "Our God," says the author to the Hebrews, "is a consuming fire", and the context in which that saying occurs is remarkable. It comes after a contrast between the old Sinai "that burned with fire" and the new Mount Zion, the heavenly Jerusalem. Nevertheless even in this happy situation of the redeemed, God is still a consuming fire. There is sound psychological insight in that judgement as well as good theological doctrine.

In religious education, therefore, it is well to begin with what is known and to cast our knowledge into that general form which is doctrine. For there is psychological doctrine, biological doctrine, and mathematical doctrine, as well as theological. It is quite a mistake to treat "doctrine" as if it were a copyright of theologians. In expounding the principles which underlie the love relationship between persons with its ambivalence of unity and individuality, of the sense of freedom and the sense of restraint, of the fullest enjoyment and yet the fullest sense of responsibility, we have been expounding doctrine. It ought to be possible, then, to take this doctrine and apply it to our relationship to God and see whether it does not help to create in the unseen world that same sense of relationship out of which the doctrine itself arose in the world of time and sense that we know so well. There is a natural history of religion in the soul, and one way in which men have found God with greatest assurance has been in their own experience

of love. The first Epistle of John is a treatise on this very
subject.

(c) With this clue let us now look at the third of these
fundamental needs of man—the need for significance.

It is here where we become most aware of frustration and
imperfection in ourselves and in the world which we would
remould nearer to the heart's desire. It is not that we wish
to be important people but rather that we wish somehow
to count. And this desire for significance is a curious thing.
It is not satisfied simply by receiving the tribute of respect
and service from other people. We have to be genuinely
significant in our own eyes as well as in those of others. And
self-respect is much harder to achieve, for even in the people
who are consciously content with outward success there is
an unconscious dissatisfaction.[1] It is this principle which
causes men who seek satisfaction in money or in power to feel
that they never have enough. All outward satisfactions are
quantitative but the human soul is never satisfied with quantity,
and quality is something inward, not outward.

Now is not this true to the Christian doctrine of man—
seeking rest and finding none except in God, never really
contented with outwardness and yet always frustrated of
inward peace because of sin, either his own sin or the sin
of the world or both? Where this sense of frustration is
present the Christian Gospel comes with a promise of hope and
fulfilment, although not always in the way originally expected.
Where this is not present the Christian Gospel comes in as a
challenge and *produces* an awareness of sin which it is then its
concern to grapple with and resolve. And it is true to our
best psychological knowledge as well as to Christian doctrine
that there is a close integration between the experience of
love and the experience of sin.

Love makes us aware of our own imperfections as nothing
else can, and love gives us the strength to overcome them.
Love also gives us a significance which nothing else can do so

[1] Lord Reith's extraordinarily frank autobiography, *Into the Wind*, is a
variation on this theme.

fully. To realize that we mean everything to someone else is to give us a dignity in our own eyes which no multiplication of mere tokens of regard can produce. It is not surprising, therefore, that all the crude theories of atonement—that Christ's death was a ransom paid to the devil, for instance— have lost their force in this generation, because at no point do they touch human experience. We have come to see that it is the love of God that is the redeeming power in the world. Nor is it surprising that to so many people "sin" is chiefly synonymous with "sex". Sex so obviously concerns the relationship between two persons and is involved both in the best and highest experiences that we know and also in the worst. It can so easily lead to sin and frustration and betrayal, and it can also lead to happiness. St. Bernard's sermons on the Song of Solomon contain many passages which are just as true of human love as of divine love and he frankly takes the relations of the soul with God as paralleled with those of a man to his wife. This has been characteristic of one great school of mystical writers to which Catherine of Siena, Julian of Norwich, and Bernard himself belong. Yet on the other hand the same relationship forms the staple interest of the least reputable Sunday newspapers. Clearly, therefore, sound teaching about the relations of men and women is a preparation for the Gospel.

6

It is often held that the cardinal Christian doctrine is faith, and that it must be so because God is unseen and, apart from the Bible and the records of Christian experience, unknown. "Faith", therefore, is often urged as a Christian "duty", concerning something which we have got to accept on the authority of other people more knowledgeable about these matters than ourselves. But this is a complete confusion. To accept "faith" on authority is a contradiction. And yet to demand "evidence" is equally a contradiction. This dilemma is very clearly seen by intelligent persons and they are quite likely to assume that "faith" in matters Christian is an acceptance of something which you know to be untrue!

Yet faith is the most ordinary experience of mankind. No one buying a cup of coffee at a railway buffet would insist on having it analysed in order to be certain that there is no poison in it. It is very rarely that any shopkeeper feels that he must test a coin to see if it is a counterfeit. We assume that what *The Times* or the *Manchester Guardian* publish is true, even though we might have our doubts about *Pravda* and *Isvestia*. What is all this if it is not faith? The fact is that the demand for "proof" can be satisfied within only a very limited range. For the great majority of transactions we rely on faith alone. Even the financial arrangements of the world are carried on on faith, which is only another name for credit.

"Faith" then is not a doctrine, it is a practice, and as such it is quite easy to understand the necessity for it. It is nevertheless the result of a degree of evidence. Cups of coffee are not usually poisoned and therefore it is likely that this one is all right. We do not stop to find out if it is so, but probably when the Borgias were in power in Italy it might have been well to make sure. The devastating effect of the destruction of faith is seen today in countries where "security" is sought by espionage and secret police. The whole morale of a nation becomes rotten with suspicion.

There are therefore plenty of illustrations available for the normality of faith in ordinary life. Are there any such for the Christian life? The author to the Hebrews has no doubt that there are, but this is an argument hardly likely to convince the twentieth-century enquirer. Yet it is interesting that the Society of Friends in the first volume of its *Book of Discipline* gives a long catena of illustrations from modern times of men and women who "trusted in God" and who ordered their lives in accordance with that trust. But of course everything depends on who you consider God to be. If He is thought of as one who favours His own people and will grant things to Catholics which He won't give to Protestants and vice versa, that He is moody, capricious, revengeful, faith becomes a somewhat difficult problem because you never know where you stand. On the other hand if He is a God of love, why does He allow earthquakes and floods, and why does He allow wars to go on? These are all very frequent questions. What is not always noticed is that the very asking of them indicates faith of a sort. When a man says "I can't believe in a God of love allowing a man to die of cancer", it is fair to ask "In what way did you ever come to believe that God is a God of love?" Is that not faith? And what is the alternative? We can believe in a God after the old pagan pattern or we can believe in no God at all. Are these beliefs more easy or less easy to hold than the belief in God as a God of love?

It is here where the Bible is really evidential. If we follow the historical method we shall see how men arrived at the belief that God was a God of love. It was by insight into their own inmost experiences. Hosea hit upon this truth not by accident nor by some word spoken to him in the night but by brooding upon his own attitude to his erring wife. He could not destroy her because he still loved her. Was it possible then that God was in the same case with regard to people in general? Could God have a lower moral character than a man? If not, let us see how it works out if we have faith that God is a God of love. And so the hypothesis was put to the test and was seen to make far more sense of the world than any other. But the doctrine that God is love was not promulgated by a committee of theologians but was hammered out on the anvil of men's experience. And just as experience of some men created the doctrine, so the doctrine in turn can re-create the experience in other men.

CHAPTER IX

SCEPTICISM AND INFALLIBILITY

I

IT is one of the popular superstitions of the present age that science deals with things which can be proved, whereas history, philosophy, poetry, religion are concerned only with ideas and words. So rooted is this belief that the "arts" people are often intimidated by it and allow themselves to accept methods of exposition in their own studies which are strictly applicable only to the study of natural science and mathematics. Philosophers, psychologists and even theologians and poets, fearful lest they be thought to be "unscientific" (the most popular term of disparagement nowadays), adopt an esoteric vocabulary and esoteric arguments to show that they, too, are foxes with scientific tails.

Now it is a fact that spiritual things are spiritually discerned and that the truths of art or religion or philosophy are not discoverable in the same way in which the natural scientist discovers truth. We might, however, go farther and say that there are two kinds of truth—that of the scientist and that of the artist, or, again alternatively, that of the analyst and that of the person who appreciates wholeness, and each sets the standard within its own sphere. There is therefore no need whatever for the religious man to have his withers wrung because he cannot "prove" the validity of his experience to a man who has it not, any more than a lover of art should be ashamed because he cannot convince somebody else that he is looking at "a good picture". "Proof" in any context implies the existence of an alternative approach, two or three or more methods of assessing the same thing, two witnesses and not merely one, but there are whole regions of experience in which "proof" of this sort is not only impossible but also irrelevant.

But even in regions where "proof" is held to be both necessary and available are we really sure that we are not following a will-o'-the-wisp? The angles of a triangle on a plane surface add up to two right angles. That can be "proved" and nobody doubts that it is true. But here we are in the very limited region of mathematics within which proof of this sort is possible because certain data are assumed at the outset. Euclid himself began with postulates—"let it be granted". Yet even here a statement may be true so long as we remain within this closed circle and yet may be false as regards the world outside. It is a schoolboy joke that by the laws of simple proportion if two men can put up a wall in seven hours 100,000 men could put it up in half a second! Yet many of the applications of mathematics and statistics to the affairs of human life may be no less fallacious than this—true on paper and quite untrue in fact.

Here then is one *caveat* to the blind acceptance of scientific infallibility. But there is another. In natural science as distinct from mathematics, we discover that more is required than "proof" of the mathematical type. I say, for example, that the action of sulphuric acid on zinc is to give off hydrogen. It is a fact that comes quite early in any elementary text-book on chemistry. But how do I know it? Every time I have done this experiment the same result happens and this is held to "prove" the statement in the book. It is an alternative approach. But how many times has this experiment to be done in order to be sure that the conclusion is a right one— fifty, a hundred, a thousand? Why should we stop at any one of these numbers? Moreover, why should I be content to do the experiment only in England? Might not the result be different if it was tried out at the Equator or at the North Pole? What is it, therefore, that makes one content with evidence gathered only in England and to stop at, say, half a dozen experiments?

Whatever it is, it is certainly not *certainty*. It is guess-work

—justifiable guess-work, if you will, but still guess-work, no matter how probable it may be. And lest it be thought that this is mere quibbling, we need only call to mind how many scores and hundreds of experiments must have been done in laboratories in this and other countries on the chemical composition of the atmosphere, all of them confirming the traditional answer of oxygen, nitrogen, carbon dioxide and water vapour. Yet the day came when that was outmoded by new experiments demonstrating the existence of inert gases in addition to those already known. And then, too, we have the revolution in Newtonian physics which has taken place in our own generation, neatly hit off by the satirist in an addendum to Pope's well-known epigram:

Nature and Nature's laws lay hid in Night:
God said *Let Newton be!* and all was Light.

(Pope)

It did not last: the Devil howling *Ho!*
Let Einstein be! restored the status quo!

(J. C. Squire)

The upshot of all this is that J. H. Newman's well-known distinction between inference and assent which he worked out in his *Essay in Aid of a Grammar of Assent* (1870) is as valid in natural science as elsewhere. My statement that sulphuric acid on zinc gives off hydrogen is an inference from a limited number of examples. If it is taken to be more than that, if I use it as a "fact" on the basis of which I can confidently do further experiments without having to repeat this one, I am making an act of faith. I am believing that this reaction will happen anywhere and at any time although I am not in a position so to make it happen. I have given assent and committed myself to something which I cannot "prove". And the further question arises—why should I commit myself at this particular point rather than at any other? What is it that decides me to stop just here and make a flying leap to a generalization? Is it not a risk? It is the willingness to take this risk and the knowledge of the right time to take it that distinguishes the great scientist from the mere plodder.

2

This is not irrelevant to the subject of this book. Children and not they alone are in the habit of asking, "Is it true?" and if the subject is religion they still expect the same sort of answer that they require from a railway time-table or a scientific magazine. And there are those who claim to be able to give precisely this kind of information. Fundamentalist preachers, Catholic apologists and certain types of Modernists believe that they have all the answers and have no diffidence in giving them. A friend of mine once asked a Jesuit theologian if he knew when the wafer of the Sacrament ceased to be the body of Christ. He scarcely meant the question seriously, but the answer came pat—"When it enters the great intestine". Fundamentalists, as we have already seen, have done violence to all zoological and physiological evidence over the question of Jonah and the whale, and the word "miracle" is over-worked in order to provide the same *kind* of assurance that other people find in scientific proof.

The old Puritan divines were as self-assured on their side as the Catholics on theirs and the melancholy history of heresy trials, Catholic and Protestant, is a witness to men's unholy unwillingness *not* to know. The judges in these cases are as much on trial as the defendants, for they would shrink eternity to a span and comprehend the unfathomable with a plumb-line of their own contriving. And this is as true of modern Continental theologians and their English fellow-travellers as it ever was of other schools of thought. However, it cannot be too often pointed out that in spiritual matters scientific exactitude is the surest indication of insensitiveness, for it belongs to a sphere that is alien from that to which it is applied. You may write a book with a pen and you may write a book with a purpose but no argument is possible between categories that are so completely different.

Does this, therefore, mean that there is no exactness possible in religion, that truth is all a matter of conjecture, and that vague feelings can be a substitute for thought? We have already seen the fallacy in the emphasis on "atmosphere" as the criterion of reality. It does, however, mean that there are not only different truths but also different kinds of truth and that scientific accuracy is only one of them. Truth and accuracy are by no means convertible terms, and in our religious education it is most important to observe the distinction between them.

Exactitude is an intellectual concept. We have our own means of measuring it, and there is a sense of satisfaction in being able to control our material to this extent. Anybody with a graduated scale can give the exact size of a wall or the height of a head of mercury, for these objects, including the scale itself, are things that can be touched and handled and compared. But how can we measure intelligence, or beauty, or wisdom, or goodness, or integrity? The so-called "educational" psychologists have their tests of intelligence and up to a point they are most helpful. It is when they are considered able to tell the whole story instead of only part of it that their very accuracy makes them untrue to life. There have also been invented what are called "personality" tests which still further attempt to weigh the imponderable. A few years ago the University of Indiana came out with a whole battery of tests which would demonstrate whether the person tested was or was not a Christian, and, if so, how far his Christianity extended. The education of the emotions itself has been studied by means of questionnaires and statistics in order to "evaluate" the attitude of some hundreds of people towards art and music and so to find guidance for the future for everybody. In most of these attempts not only to define but accurately to measure the essentially indefinable and unmeasurable the limit of absurdity was very soon reached, yet they were no more absurd than the slick judgements of people lightly tinged with science who apply their own yard-stick to spiritual matters the nature of which they have not taken the trouble to understand.

Applied, therefore, to human affairs, exactitude can be pursued only by the elimination of those emotional and unpredictable factors which make a man a man and not a machine. Human nature hates to feel baffled by anything, and any method will be snatched at which appears to offer certainty because certainty gives the control that is desired. Nevertheless such an attitude is fundamentally sceptical, for it is a disbelief in the essential nature of that which we are studying. Every type of truth has a law of its own being, and to ignore that law, in the attempt to make one kind of experience act as the standard of another, is to be in the profoundest sense of the term "unscientific". It is imposing upon our material alien standards which we ourselves bring from elsewhere, and so in effect disqualifying ourselves from recognizing the truth when we see it. The mathematical friend who informed me as a jest that Wordsworth was "wrong" when he wrote of King's College Chapel

> and scoop'd into ten thousand cells
> Where light and shade repose, where music dwells
> Lingering

because "there are at most only fifteen hundred. I've counted them", gave a unique illustration of this misfitting of judgements. It was "the pen and the purpose" controversy again! Scepticism may thus arise from two apparently different causes. It may arise from the application of irrelevant standards which are thus seen not to fit, and hence not the standard but the subject is held to be at fault. It may arise from the very inability to apply any known standard at all, and therefore it is held that the subject must be unreal, a subjective delusion of the mind. This is how many people speak of religion. They come to it with their minds made up as to their idea of the truths of religion, and as by that standard it is found wanting, it can be dismissed. And there are no people who are greater victims of this self-deception than scientists themselves. Let Mr. Fred Hoyle stand as the type. His *Nature of the Universe* is a most excellent book until he comes at the end to discuss Christianity. Here he applies his specialist yardstick with as little understanding of his material as any schoolboy just beginning to do science. Of a similar nature was the attitude of a woman who once told me that if she were to believe that Job never lived the *whole Bible* would be completely valueless to her. Here she was imposing upon the Bible a standard of truth brought in ready-made from elsewhere, and yet she was one of those people who hold that "the Bible should be allowed to speak for itself". A more subtle form of the same attitude is that of the man who tells you that he can't believe in a good God because a good God would not allow earthquakes or wars to happen.

Two offshoots of this fundamental scepticism are cynicism and fatalism. They are both attitudes of mind based on a disillusionment of their own making. The cynic's disillusionment is bitter and the fatalist's is either neutral or self-pitying, and both of them are deficiency diseases of the mind. They do not find what they are looking for and they do not ask themselves whether they are looking in the right place or for the right thing.

> Ah love, could thou and I with Fate conspire
> To grasp this sorry scheme of things entire
>   Would we not shatter it to bits and then
> Remould it nearer to the heart's desire?

Or, if we might take a more modern example, here is the soliloquy of "Mimnermus in Church":

> You promise heavens free from strife,
>   Pure truth and perfect change of will,
> But sweet, sweet is this human life,
>   So sweet that I would breathe it still.
> Your chilly stars I can forego,
> This warm kind world is all I know.[1]

3

In affairs of religion infallibility is, as we have seen, simply scepticism by another name. It occurs where the intellectual factor in belief is exalted to a position quite out of

[1] by William (Johnson) Cory.

proportion to its real importance. The satisfaction of the intellect is considered to be equivalent to the satisfaction of the whole man. It is intrinsically a disbelief in truth and an assumption that truth requires to be hedged about with "safeguards" lest it disappear altogether. The very word "safeguard" implies that truth is not considered to be strong enough to stand up for itself. When those who use the term are possessed of the instruments of coercion the safeguards become far more important than the truth they are supposed to secure.

But infallibility is a quite impossible category for limited human intelligences, except within a very narrow circle. A man may be infallible as an interpreter of the rules of a game, he may be infallible as a mathematician or as a lawyer, but to claim infallibility in the affairs of God, who is from everlasting to everlasting, is to fall into the sin of that familiarity which is contempt. The great scientist would never claim infallibility for his system. For new truth may at any time make ancient good uncouth. The future may and almost certainly will outmode the present. But it is the characteristic of infallibility that it is concerned not at all with the future nor even with the present. It is wholly concerned with the past, for it assumes that the circle of revelation is closed. It must indeed make that assumption, otherwise it cannot be sure of its control over the material with which it is concerned. Moreover, by the very nature of things it can be concerned only with particulars, for the universal cannot be considered as confined to the past alone. Yet even then the hypothesis of infallibility can apply only to such particulars as are already known. The theologian who defends infallibility is therefore in the same plight as the scientist—he has to be content to draw an inference and to go outside the circle of his infallibility to justify himself for drawing the line at this point rather than at that. Infallibility never operates outside the circle of its devotees—a fact which in itself destroys its claim.

But this is not the whole story. Other causes of the acceptance of infallibility are fear, insecurity and self-flattery.

Some men are so afraid of the risks of a healthy agnosticism that they will accept almost any authority as their anchor. Infallibility is the evaporation of faith rather than its demonstration. And of course it provides a subtle way of paying a compliment to oneself without the appearance of conceit, yet in effect it is pride masquerading as humility. It looks the same as assurance; in fact it is nothing of the kind. It has within it all the marks of timidity, uncertainty and indecision. It is a kind of cutting one's losses—being content with what we already have and what can easily be grasped, fearfully laying up the talent in a napkin so that it is there, whole, intact and unfruitful. How can it be otherwise, for it is an externalizing of an inward quality, not a sacrament of it but a substitute for it. If we view truth as the goal of a journey, this is an attempted short cut to that goal, a desire to be done with striving and with hope deferred, and an insistence on sight instead of being content with faith. It is the surest sign that a man is not at home in the spiritual world.

4

I have hinted that religious experience is more akin to æsthetic appreciation than to logical reasoning, and that the attempt to make it mathematically definable is bound to issue in scepticism in the form of either disbelief or infallibility. There are plenty of analogies at hand. How, for instance, are we to describe a Highland landscape after a rainy day? We may attempt it in words and use all the adjectives we can muster to describe the dozen shades of blue in the sky and in the distance, but it all fails just because we are trying to be exact in one medium in order to capture exactness in another. The only way in which it can be done is to abandon altogether the attempt at statement and to use suggestion instead. Take for example Coleridge's *Hymn before Sunrise* and see how he describes Mont Blanc—

> thou, most awful form
> Risest from forth thy silent sea of pines

> How silently! Around thee and above
> Deep is the air and dark, substantial, black,
> An ebon mass: methinks thou piercest it
> As with a wedge: but when I look again
> It is thine own calm home, thy crystal shrine,
> Thy habitation from eternity.

It would be very difficult to draw a picture of the mountain from the materials furnished here by Coleridge, and yet has he not suggested the whole thing far better than any photograph could have done?

Or take Milton's "description" of Satan:

> talking to his nearest mate
> With head uplift above the wave, and eyes
> That sparkling blazed; his other parts besides
> Prone on the flood, extended long and large
> Lay floating many a rood.

A picture of this even by Gustave Doré, who specialized in drawing the undrawable, gives an infinitely less effective impression than the language of suggestion used by Milton. In Milton's account there is "nothing to get hold of" and yet the whole thing is there. There is all the difference in the world between a coloured photograph and a painting of the same scene. The one is exact and literal and shows everything, but has no "feeling" in it at all. The other is impressionistic and while blurring the details gives you the thing as a whole. We come therefore to the unexpected paradox that the farther we appear to go away from reality the nearer we come to it. This is the difference between great literature and poor literature. Poor literature ignores form and is concerned only with content. Such, for example, are Ella Wheeler Wilcox's verses and (for a different reason) Lamb's *Tales from Shakespeare*. In great literature form and content go together. It is the literature of suggestion and metaphor. This turning one's back upon reality and seeking out the suggestive phrase rather than the photographic description is in many ways an act of faith. The reader *may* fail to see the point and the writer may be misunderstood. Yet, as we have seen, every search for truth, whether in literature or in science, requires just such an act of faith as this, and it is only on those conditions that truth can ever be found.

On the higher levels of life, therefore, truth is not a proposition but an experience. It is something that is intuitively grasped. But intuition is not an alternative to thought nor a substitute for it. It is the very culmination of thought and it is not exhausted by our own experience of it. An essential point of an experience is the sense that there is something more beyond. It may come as a result of thinking but it is not an addition to thinking. Rather it is the point where thinking fuses and becomes something different. It is like the difference between intimate companionship and falling in love. Precisely the same factors are present but a point has been reached at which an altogether new situation is set up which can by no means be accounted for by a mere assessment of the factors present. As " Abt Vogler " has it:

But here is the finger of God, a flash of the will that can,
Existent behind all laws, that made them and, lo, they are!
And I know not if, save in this, such gift be allowed to man,
That out of three sounds he frame not a fourth sound, but a
    star.

This is particularly true in the case of persons. The truth about persons can never be a mere assessment of qualities. These things no doubt come into it, but appreciation of the whole man rather than an analysis of his virtues is the final standard.

Faith therefore is needed. And, in this context, the opposite of faith is detachment. This detachment is the cause of the ready use of labels to sum up a man's character. We call him a Communist, a bourgeois or a bigot or a fool and so doing dispose of him. This is the same kind of short cut which we have noticed in the case of infallibility. It saves the trouble of further thought. It keeps judgement at a low level and the quick answer is the one most acceptable.

5

Anselm's slogan—*credo ut intelligam*—I believe in order that I may understand—is the sum of the matter. It is not more knowledge that we need but a different attitude. Undue reliance upon knowledge leads, as we have seen, to scepticism, for sooner or later the discovery is made that there is no absolute certainty along this line, everything is an approximation. Increase of knowledge, moreover, inhibits emotion and so makes action all the more difficult. Jane Addams, the great American social reformer, was at one period of her life concerned with investigations into cruelty to animals. When she found that she could look unmoved at a bullfight she felt that the time had come to stop collecting evidence and to allow her original sympathy to take control.

It is wholeness and not quantity that matters if we would come at truth, but there are two sides to wholeness. First of all it refers to the inner principle of a thing, that which makes it what it really is. A man, for instance, can be defined as a featherless biped, or, as by Aristotle, as the only cooking animal. Both of these descriptions are true and as they each indicate uniqueness they come under the heading of good definitions. Yet we know that neither of these represents that real inward principle of humanity which is expressed by the scientific label *homo sapiens*. Reason, however, is the *characteristic* thing about mankind and is far more than just one quality among many, even though the others are also unique. It represents that which makes a man a man.

In the second place, wholeness has reference not only to the subject being studied but also to the student. We understand a thing fully only when we bring to it our whole selves. The intellect is one part of ourselves, and its concern also is for wholeness, of the first not of the second kind. It insists on reducing a subject to order and on imposing upon it a pattern of its own. As children we traced patterns in the wallpaper of our room which were never intended by its designer, and we continue doing this sort of thing all through life. It is what the Germans call a *Gestalt* mechanism. But just because of this habit of mind we tend to hold that the pattern traced by our thinking is the only important and, indeed, the only pattern. Sociologists impose their own pattern upon social phenomena, economists likewise, and psychologists have often claimed possession of the whole outgoings of a man's personality. Yet these are all partial judgements and amid so much that is contradictory we may well ask ourselves where is the real man. The discovery of man is the motif in Ibsen's *Peer Gynt*:

> where was my real self,
> Complete and true—the Peer who bore
> The stamp of God upon his brow?

and he is given the answer by the woman who loves him—

> In my faith, in my hope and in my love.

She has believed in him all the while and has not been put off by his foibles or the variety of his interests. She alone has known the real man because she alone was concerned with him as a person, irrespective of class, occupation, creed or anything else. She believed in him and therefore she understood.

6

Now let us bring all this argument into connection with the rest of this book.

It has been held that the cure for scepticism of any sort is wholeness. This is perhaps more true of religion than of any other activity of man. Religion is concerned with a man's relation to the unseen world, and the Christian religion is concerned with that relationship as interpreted by the historical events recorded in the Bible and particularly in the New Testament. But wholeness can be both subjective and objective, that is to say, it is concerned both with the believer and with what he believes. As to the believer, it has already been noted that Christian religious experience has not one but five aspects. It involves knowledge, feeling, choice, conduct and belonging. The isolation of any one of these from the others is bound sooner or later to land us in scepticism or in the claim of infallibility. Healthy-minded religion involves all five.

As to the subject matter of Christianity, a problem arises for our generation which has not been present before in quite the same way. We find that one result of the acceptance of the historical view of the Bible has been a sectional attitude towards the Scriptures.

In my house there is an old Primitive Methodist loving-cup. It is a large, two-handled vessel which was handed round during the special service known as a "love-feast". On one side of it are the words "Love Feast", and on the other there is a picture of a flying angel with a trumpet and the words "Prepare to meet thy God". Now the old folk who used this cup had no doubt at all that the words were written for *them* and were a warning to them. Every part of the Bible was equally important with every other part, for the message of the whole was addressed to the worshippers in their village chapel and to their contemporaries outside.

Nowadays, however, we know and some of their successors know that these words were really addressed by Amos to the citizens of Israel in the year 753 B.C. and that in order to understand them we must study the situation with which Amos was dealing. But this historical reference wipes out the present-day reference which to the older generation was absolutely vital. It separates the contemporary message from its application today, and this is a far more serious "splitting up" of the Bible than the separation of the various documents in Genesis. And this study of the historical situation has gone ahead and in some places has become less and less concerned for the lives and souls of the men of our own time. Consequently there has been a growth of scepticism even among those who are ardent students of the Bible after the modern fashion. It expresses itself not in disbelief of the Bible—which was the scepticism in those earlier days of verbal inspiration —but in a belief that the historical reference is all that there is to it.

The problem, therefore, is how can we restore *wholeness* to our study of the Bible. Can it become in our day for us what it was for our forefathers? There are various wrong answers to this question. One is that it requires the abandonment of the historical method. Another is that we must take at any rate the Old Testament allegorically, and I have already discussed this argument earlier. These are both unscholarly attitudes, for the right answer must be that which accepts the historical method but sees it as a means of reconstructing the human situation with which the prophets and others dealt and which remains essentially the same wherever the deepest problems of human life are concerned.

Thus we return to the argument of an earlier chapter concerning the right use of the Bible. The historical method, wisely pursued, is the best argument against a foolish theory of infallibility and the best prophylactic against scepticism, for it recognizes that ordinary human life and experience are the stuff out of which history is made, and that they are as relevant to the interpretation of the Bible as is the best historical scholarship.

CHAPTER X

THE CHRISTIAN COMMUNITY

I

THERE is no aspect of the Christian faith more difficult for religious education than the place and meaning of the Church. This is due partly to its apparent *lack* of difficulty. Church history is, or can be, interesting and indeed exciting, and a period such as that of the Reformation is full of colour and movement. Belonging to a church has certain obvious benefits. There is the sense of a historical community, and at the local level there are things to do and people to meet. All this is easy to bring home to children by both precept and practice. But, as we know, the Christian idea of the Church comprehends much more than this.

The local church itself, however, is not always very helpful. To some people the church is scarcely more than a club for religious purposes and in some churches the enquirer can obtain a balance sheet showing the annual turnover and the income required to keep the business solvent. What, in such a setting, can children learn about the church which would be any different from what they would learn about a co-opera-tive store or a cinema club? There are others to whom the church is a convenient pressure group to compel politicians and administrators to let its members have their own way in questions of education, divorce, foreign policy and indeed everything under the sun. There is no great element of edification affecting religious education to be obtained here.

Then there are those into whose eyes comes a far-away look when they talk about the Church. It is a supernatural society, the body of Christ, His spotless bride, the custodian of the oracles of God, the blessed company of the redeemed, and a few more romantic titles, none of which seems to tally with what the outsider can see for himself in "St. Agatha's Parish Church" or "High Street Methodists". In this case the children will rightly want to know just what it is that we are talking about. When we say that Jesus founded the Church, where is the Church that He founded? Did He found the R.C. church at the corner and Baptists near the station and the Plymouth Brethren by the post office? These are all that the enquirer has to go upon when he thinks about the matter at all, and when an adherent of any one of these bodies talks large about the claims of "the Church" we must not be surprised if it appears to the outsider to be no more than salesmanship with nothing in the shop to sell. And things are made still more complicated when we find the Roman Catholic section utterly convinced that they alone are the "true Church" and the Protestant Truth Society equally convinced that Romanists are little more than pagans, and little groups of Strict Baptists positive that to them alone have the oracles of God been committed.

These then are the lions in the path of religious education, and they are so formidable that "the Church" as part of the Christian Gospel is often left out altogether. It is this which caused the English Education Act of 1870 to lay down that in religious teaching in public elementary schools "no religious catechism or religious formulary distinctive of any particular denomination" was ever to be used. It is this which has resulted in the secularization of national education in Canada and the United States.

Nevertheless the matter cannot be left there. Even if in North America there can as yet be no agreement concerning religion in the schools, and religious education has to be done by the churches themselves, the question still arises whether there can be teaching about the Church *as such* rather than propaganda for the particular denomination. No useful

N

purpose can be served by clouding the subject with sentimentality. The bride of Christ needs to be told that she is

A creature not too good
For human nature's daily food

just as the ecclesiastical club-man has to be reminded that this
is no ordinary community but is the society for which Christ
died and is His agent for the redemption of the world.

2

There are certain points that have to be kept clearly in
mind. The Church is an integral part of the Gospel. It is
not a society of people brought into existence to propagate
the Christian faith. It is itself part of the Christian faith. We
must avoid the idea that Jesus was simply a teacher and that
after His death the Church carried on His teaching. In a very
real sense the Church *is* His teaching.

It is in this sense that it can be said that Jesus "founded"
the Church. Yet it is at this very point that religious education so easily becomes propaganda. Thus it is held by some
that Jesus established their own particular denomination just
as we find it today, that He laid down the rules and organization, just as man might establish a college or any other
institution. If this is admitted in one case, why not in all
cases? There is in fact no *one* Church at all. There are a
whole lot of "churches". Is then the conclusion that Jesus
founded all these denominations? To the intelligent church
member this, no doubt, is an absurd question, but looked at
impartially and from outside is it so absurd after all? At any
rate, it is an issue which we have to remember all the time
in our religious education. What we can say with truth is
that the existence of a Christian community within which
the enabling power of Christ is believed to be present, in
which the Christian virtues can grow and be practised and
which is a perpetual witness to the Will of God for the world,
certainly follows from, or rather is inherent in, the life and

work of Christ. "Christianity" is not a body of doctrine which we preach: it is the name given to the corporate life and witness of men who are in personal avowed loyalty to Jesus Christ. The Church, no doubt, is wider than this, for it includes very many people who are not so dedicated, but who follow afar off. But there must also be in every generation a solid core of dedicated spirits among whom Christ comes alive again and is made known to men. The Old Testament word is "the remnant". It is through them that the Church is able to perform its peripheral tasks as well as its main function.

There is thus a distinction to be drawn, but it is not a dual standard of conduct, not the distinction between a professional and salaried body and an unprofessional body, not the distinction between "lay" and "ordained", or "secular" and "regular". It is the distinction which we have already noted between the function of evangelism and the function of diffusion. The Church has been concerned with the diffusion of Christian principles and ideas in the secular world, and many reformers have done the work of Christ in this regard without themselves being convinced or even nominal Christians. But the second function has been to convert men from sin to a life of righteousness and so to have a body of fully committed persons to carry on the work into the next generation.

In bringing a consideration of the Church into any scheme of Christian education we have to allow for both of these concepts, and the emphasis on one or the other will vary according to a person's experience and age. The Boy Scout Movement, for example, and the Girl Guides are based on Christian principles, and a great deal of social service is of the same character. Of such the word of Jesus is apt: "he that is not against us is for us". This may be a warning to those earnest Christians who feel that absolute commitment is the right demand for every person at every age and at every stage of experience. They ignore in this context as in others the natural laws of the soul's growth into the full Christian faith. Moreover, as far as England is concerned, this diffusionist aim is about as far as teachers in the council schools are justified in going. It is common to all denominations and is exclusively characteristic of none. For millions of children it represents the only connection that they will ever have with the Church. For them, whether we like it or not, the school is the only church they know. It is not the whole story, and it is not even the more important part of the story, but the rest is the task of the Church itself rather than the school. It is the Church's particular business to seek to create convinced Christians, to offer training in worship, to give guidance in personal religion, to order and sustain a corporate witness before the world, to care for the ministry of the word and sacraments and to be vitally concerned with the original documents of the faith and with the continuing testimony down the ages.

There are certain characteristics to be noted which the Christian community shares with other communities, such as schools. There is, for instance, the sense of being together. This for many adolescent church-goers is the main and often the only reason why they come at all. In the church they meet other like-minded people but just as they might meet them in a boys' club or a football club. This is not much of a motive if it stays at this point, but it is a genuine motive, it is perfectly natural and sensible, it is often the same as that to which a surprisingly large number of adult members would have to confess if they were challenged; but above all it is a beginning from which further progress can be made. If education is a social thing there must be some means whereby people can meet, and it is useless to expect idealism to come up of itself without any stages of growth.

Then, too, the group offers an opportunity for service. Much of modern education suffers from being too intellectualized, but it takes all sorts to make a world, and to define education according to the interest of one sort alone is to do violence to the others. Education is concerned not only with reading and writing but also with doing things and doing them for other people and doing them together. Our secondary schools are often inspiring examples of the opportunity given by corporate life to render effective service. All kinds of good causes flourish in schools, and help for them is often better organized than anywhere outside. The Church also is a society of this kind. Isolated goodwill is good as far as it goes and personal service is also good, but there needs to be a fellowship in order to carry through any long-continued scheme of service. And that fellowship is at its best when it is informed by an intelligible common purpose intense enough to sink personal differences. This was discovered in relief work by the Society of Friends, a Christian body less given to organization than any. Well-directed common effort was infinitely more effective than the efforts of multitudes of free-lance enthusiasts.[1] The Church can thus gather up all the inchoate goodwill of people and give them an opportunity to fulfil their desires in the best possible way.

3

These are two obvious characteristics of almost any community. There are two others, however, more especially concerning the Christian community, which are not quite so obvious and which require a greater recognition.

The Christian community, while it has the character of a voluntary society to which a man may belong or not as he chooses, has also the quality of being a society of unlikes as well as of likes. Given the central fact of loyalty to Christ as the unifying factor, we then notice that there are within it people of all ages, temperaments and abilities, as well as people of all classes, races and nations. When Paul pointed out that in Christ there cannot be Greek and Jew, barbarian, Scythian, bondman, freeman, he was not so much giving a description as issuing a warning. It could not have been easy for all these exclusive groups in the early Church to get on happily together, and it illustrates the tremendous power

[1] See Roger Wilson. *Authority, Leadership and Concern* (Swarthmore Lecture, 1949). It is an admirable handling of this theme and incidentally an excellent exposition of the Christian view of authority.

of the grace of Christ that they managed it so well. There was nothing else in the ancient world which managed it at all. And it is not easy even nowadays for intellectuals and manual workers, old people and young, traditionalists and progressives, to live and work together in any kind of society, political, cultural or neighbourly. There are tensions within a miscellaneous group of this kind which require a very powerful common loyalty or a crisis to overcome.

Yet the Christian community is precisely a society of that kind, and the right word to use here is not "overcome" but "utilize". For tension is the very breath of life to the Christian community, and a segregated society of likes is its negation. This fact is not always grasped, and in these days there is often too much segregation within the Church— women's meetings, boys' clubs, girls' clubs, junior church, and so on. These have their essential place in the scheme of corporate life, but they can easily tend to avoid tension rather than to sublimate it. But part of religious education is to train people to live together in a society of differences. Such variety has a romantic attractiveness until we come to work it out in practice. Yet it is vitally necessary to work it out in practice, bearing and forbearing with one another in love, because it is the inability or even the unwillingness to do this which so bitterly divides the nations of the earth at this time. And tension can be found at both levels, that of the local church with people you meet every day and that of the denomination as a whole. To insist on uniformity of witness even to the same loyalty would negate that loyalty. Paul's implication is that " in Christ" these distinctions are neither eliminated nor ignored but transcended.

A further characteristic of the Christian community is that it puts a person into a historical succession. So also does a school, a college, a regiment and many other institutions. One of our big banks proudly displays the date of its foundation in 1677 and a great publishing house makes good publicity out of the fact that it began in 1724. It adds dignity to a person to feel that he has a long and honourable ancestry, and while a few men can achieve this in their own personal history it is available to all by belonging to a society. In this there is an enlargement of the spirit and at the same time a sense of discipline. There are things that are "done" and things that are "not done" when you belong to any institution, and you accept them as badges of distinction rather than as limitations on your freedom. The Christian community is of this nature also. It has a history built up out of all nations and centuries and peoples and tongues. It is a history of development, for new truths are continually being discovered and old truths are seen in a new light. It too brings an enlargement of the spirit and a discipline of life. It too has its sense of things "done" and "not done", and if the society appears to men to be something desirable the incentive to strive to attain its standard is already provided. Here, however, as in other contexts, it is not the community as an end in itself but the community as setting forth Christ that is the incentive. To belong to a society of which He is Lord and Leader is the right way to view the approach to church membership.

4

The relations of the community with the individual raise some important issues for education. No person can grow spiritually unless he has both a measure of solitude and a measure of corporate activity. Action and contemplation are both needed. With older people there is a tension here, but with younger people it is more often a matter of rhythm—the one alternating with the other. In many ways today it is privacy that is the more difficult to obtain, but at all ages of life and in all ages of history a compromise has been possible. The secret society or the privileged society, even if not secret, provides a sort of vicarious privacy over against those who are not members of it. Robert Louis Stevenson's juvenile "lantern bearers"[1] who carried a dark lantern under their coats at night and showed it only to members of the band

[1] In the collection *Across the Plains*.

were recognizing both privacy and community. The use of Scout badges, or indeed badges of any sort, again marks both similarity and difference. No doubt one of the attractions of the mystery religions was this same double service. All religions have had their little groups, cells and communities which satisfy these two needs at one and the same time.

Religion has been described as the flight of the alone to the alone, and there is truth in this. But in Christianity this "aloneness" is not solitariness even though it may mean solitude. It is coloured by the sense of companionship of an innumerable host of witnesses. For the Christian community is not confined to people here and now, it is one with its history, for it is believed that the immortals really are immortal, alive and still concerned with their main loyalty. The old name given to them is "the Church triumphant" as opposed to "the Church militant" here on earth. It is not a very happy name, for it suggests that immediately after death all hopes are realized and all promises fulfilled. This is not New Testament teaching. The author of Hebrews is clear that "they without us shall not be made perfect" and "us" refers to a community that is still going on. The existence of this invisible host provides that sense of solidarity which helps a man in his temptation to realize that he is not alone.

The Christian community, therefore, and the private life of the individual help one another, and each is important. The life of the group, the common loyalty, the common heritage of the Bible, the sense of being part of a historic company, and the expression of experience in the hymns of the Church all give form to a man's private life. They prevent our moods tyrannizing over us. Here are also the consolations of solitude, and solitude is needed in order fully to appropriate them. In our time, when mechanical aids of every sort combine to deprive a man of his privacy, it is valuable to belong to a society which requires solitude for the full flowering of the human spirit and at the same time can fill up that solitude with spiritual meaning so that it is not an empty void but a well-furnished retreat.

Conversely the fruits of solitude enrich the heritage of the community. Personal religion helps to disinfect our social activities from egotism and from the tendency to allow activities to stand proxy for virtues. Constantly to be able to stand back from our work and see it in the light of God's eternal purposes and of the long Christian witness down the ages is to graduate in the school of humility. It makes our gifts serviceable to other men without corrupting ourselves. Our Lord Himself in the wilderness, Paul in Arabia, Francis in the Portiuncula, Luther in the Wartburg, and Bunyan in Bedford jail have brought out of their silence great good for all the world.

5

The development of the Gospel did not cease with Paul or with Luther. In later ages men have discovered more and more of its nature, and as the flower has unfolded we are able to know more about it than when it was in the bud. There is a continuity of revelation. Unfortunately, however, two assumptions are often made which render this position ineffective. One is that these later doctrinal discoveries or inventions were already there *in that form* in the beginning, and that they owe their authority not to a living and developing witness but to the statements of early historians and writers. The other is that discoveries made, say, by later English denominations are in a quite different category from those made within those spheres that are styled "Catholic" because they are a "departure from the main stream of Christian tradition".

Here we are in a realm of keen controversy, and quite often find ourselves besieged by arguments that are not amenable to evidence. They rest largely on feeling, and where feeling comes into a matter that is essentially historical it determines our interpretation of history. Nevertheless, this controversy appears in education and is very relevant even to the demand that the State should pay the whole cost of denominational teaching in the schools. If denominational teaching had no negative side to it, if we could assume that no denomination ever desired to "unchurch" (as the saying is) another denomination, there might be as little harm in denominational teaching of religion as there is in the denominational teaching of science or of geography, where by "denomination" we mean school of thought. But unfortunately some kinds of denominational teaching include an insistence that the whole truth is on one side alone. For this reason children may not join with children of other churches in school assembly, and denominationalism of this kind issues in segregation into groups. Where the schools are the schools of the nation, it is hardly reasonable that this attitude should be supported by public funds. The proper place for it (if there is any place) is within the domestic circle of the denomination concerned.

Christian teaching, however, is very definitely concerned with the affirmation that the spirit of God has not ceased to lead men into new truth. This is admitted in the case of natural science, but it is equally true even in the sphere of religion. We have seen how the discovery of the historical method of studying the Bible has illuminated the life and times of Christ to our generation in a way which has been hid ever since the second century. There never was a time when the study of Christianity could be made so educationally interesting as it is today.

This has been as true a revelation as anything written or done in the earlier centuries and this has been the great contribution to our knowledge of God made by the Protestant churches of the last two generations. As revealers of the truth of Christianity Robertson Smith, George Adam Smith and Adolf Deissmann have their place along with Augustine, Aquinas and Calvin, for if Christianity is a historical religion, the historians and critics are as important as the philosophers and theologians. The copyright of any one denomination as the sole publisher of the Gospel has long since run out.

The real dividing lines between Christians today cut across all denominations. The Greek Orthodox Church, lacking the devisive influence of a Papacy, has in these days realized a closer affinity with the Church of England than with the Church of Rome. The Church of England and the Free Churches have come much closer together and have learned from one another. The distinctive feature in each denomination is appreciated and in some measure provided for in all the others and, largely through the work of the Student Christian Movement, the progressive people everywhere are more at home in each other's churches than they used to be.

Yet denominations continue, and the only way to be loyal to the Church of Christ is to be loyal to one of its branches. Christianity is chosen because a man feels it to be true, but the grounds on which a denomination is chosen or cherished are nowadays far more domestic and unexciting than they used to be. The chief thing is that, whatever the motive for joining a particular society, the motive for joining any society at all should be a sense of conviction that it is the Christian Church itself which is the real centre of our loyalty. We cannot serve it except by serving some company of worshipping Christians, but this company itself has to serve the Church of Christ: it is no more an end in itself than is the individual member. It therefore provides the individual with opportunities of service, one aim of which is to make the denomination itself more worthy of the calling to which Christ has summoned all His people. Thus the critic of the Church who is nevertheless working within the Church may be a more loyal member than the complacent person who believes that his church can do no wrong. Denominations, Catholic and Protestant, may have to die that the Church may live.

To belong to a church, therefore, is a discipline of the spirit. It means giving one's loyalty to this group rather than to that, but it does not, or ought not to, imply any despite to the groups to which one does not belong. And this expression of conviction for oneself combined with perfect courtesy towards other people who have chosen differently is the "condition precedent" for any uniting of the churches together. The people who are of no use in this matter are those who believe themselves to be showing broadmindedness by seeing good in all and refusing to join any, and also those who, already members of some church, feel that a loosening of loyalty to their own communion will commend them to others.

But differences which are differences of loyalty cannot be solved except by persons who themselves know what loyalty really means. By joining a society you take over not only its goodwill but also its badwill (if there is such a word), just as by being an Englishman you are proud of the abolition of the slave trade but ashamed of the opium wars in China. Yet you cannot take credit for the one and contract out of the other. But this identification, this discipline, this tension, is all part of the price we pay not only for progress but also for insight, and to seek to avoid it is to make the great refusal. And every denomination, Catholic and Protestant, is as imperfect as any other; no good can come of pretending to ourselves that it is otherwise. Unfortunately in England the choice of denomination is complicated by social factors. The Church of England is socially higher than the Free Churches, and there is an even more subtle social snobbery in the eyes of some people with regard to the Roman Church. It could be argued that this makes the discipline of joining the Free Churches still more exacting, but it could equally well be argued the other way round, in that there is more to live down in a church that is socially more acceptable!

All churches are imperfect, and whichever we join we shall have to bear the brand of its imperfections. But this does not mean that denominations are somehow in themselves sinful, that our divisions are intrinsically "unhappy", and that if only we had been good Christians in the past there never would have been any "denominations". This is quite incapable of proof. There appear to have been sectional groups even in the apostolic church. Some were of Paul, some of Cephas, some of Apollos and some "of Christ".[1] If what is called "Christian reunion" means going back to

[1] I Corinthians i. 12.

where we were at the time of the Reformation, or still farther back to the time of the schism between East and West, and lamenting all that has happened in the interval, it does not show much regard for the operation of the Spirit of God. The gathering of Christians into various communities has exhibited and indeed made possible the wonderful variety of Christian witness, too great for any one group of men of limited knowledge and limited experience to understand or control. Did Milton, Bunyan, Wesley and Chalmers bring no enrichment of the Christian tradition? And if it be said that their witness would have been all the better had it been given in an undivided Church, this is purely wishful thinking. In *fact* it has been given in the first instance in the smaller community, but its authenticity is vouched for by the fact that it speaks to the hearts and consciences of Christian folk in *all* communities.

So far from denominations being due to human sin they have been, I believe, an absolutely necessary stage in God's education of the human race. Where division has arisen, and out of it has arisen a new authentic type of Christian witness, it is a misreading of spiritual history to assume that the part that did not change was the "true" Church and that the part that changed was schismatic. The fact is that there never has been a true Church in this sense at all. Where division of this kind arises, the old is just as "schismatic" as the new. These words "true", "schismatic", "heretical", are counters which render a partisan game possible: they have no bearing on the essential question at all.

6

The Christian society, therefore, has two fundamental values: it is the representative of the universal company of believers in Christ through whose fellowship He is made known to men—and, therefore, every Christian will wish to belong to it; it is also an aspect of Christian discipline.

It is clear from the first Epistle to the Corinthians and also from *Acts* that the real agent of evangelism was the Church itself. It was a community such as the ancient world had never seen; a community not of likes but of unlikes—bondmen and free, men and women, Jew and Gentile, rich and poor—brought together by a common loyalty to Christ rather than by a common creed about Him, and in the tension which this unlikeness set up within this common loyalty miraculous things happened. The unbeliever "will fall down on his face and worship God, declaring that God is among you indeed." (I Corinthians xiv. 25.) All attempts to go behind this and to seek for a uniformity of profession as the main essential of a Christian community have led to heresy hunting, persecution, malice and bitterness. But when men do in love bear and forbear with one another for the love that they bear to Christ, there is a spirit in the society which is altogether a new thing: it is the spirit of Christ Himself made known to them, and at the same time making this forbearance possible. How the same thing can be both effect and cause may no doubt appear to be most strange, but we are here dealing not with a philosophical investigation of how it might happen, but with a spiritual situation in which it does happen. The Christian society, where it exhibits the spirit of Christ, owes its existence to the practice of prayer.

I have spoken of "bearing and forbearing". This, however, is a very superficial level of experience. The phrase "dying to live" is much more descriptive of the Christian society than "bearing and forbearing". It is not the willingness to put up with other people that is the mark of the Christian: it is rather the willingness to be as *nothing* that they may be exalted. This is the requirement that is always made of the young: they are expected to give way to their elders, to offer unqualified obedience, and to pay their respects to age. At the same time they are expected to be adventurous, to be willing to stake all for an ideal, and to be as nothing where the need of their country or their cause is at stake. But in the Christian view of life these requirements have nothing whatever to do with age: they are required of everybody. There is an adventure for age as well as for youth. When in a church we hear someone praised for having held a particular office for fifty years, we seldom think of those who might have held it but will now never have the chance. A whole generation has been missed out. This has resulted from a refusal of age to be adventurous and to let go the seals of authority into younger hands. The disbelief that those younger people could do the work is the very negation of the Christian spirit, and because of such disbelief a church has often sunk into a purely secular type of society, in which none of the conditions in which alone Christ can be made known to men has been fulfilled.

Hence arise substitutions, some of them justifiable enough in their own place, "campaigns" to the outsider, "religion and life" weeks and missions on the one side, and on the other the substitution of a more and more rigid orthodoxy for a warm-hearted and adventurous loyalty. It is often said that education must advance along with opportunity, and that to educate people and not to open the door of opportunity creates discontent and waste. If this is true in the body politic it is equally true in the body ecclesiastic. A more thorough system of religious education will require that the teachers and the officials of such education shall exhibit at least as much of the spirit of self-sacrifice as they require of their pupils. Every teacher worthy of the name is willing thus to die that others may live.

The discipline, therefore, of the Christian society lies as squarely upon the old as upon the young. This is the factor in religion that is "caught and not taught". It is, however, not a matter of deference. For the old to defer to the young is as unwise as for the young to defer to the old. It is a matter of common loyalty, and those who have the more notable marks of that loyalty will inevitably be accepted as leaders by those who have less of them. There is no authority so absolute as that of the man who expresses in full what other people long to express in full but actually express only in part. This is an intrinsic authority, binding on all parties, for it is a recognition of the over-ruling authority of the person to whom they are all loyal.

This, however, is not the problem. The difficulty arises because to many people's minds belonging to a church necessarily involves a measure of *reproach*. It is supposed to lay upon you a limitation not only of ideas but also of fellowship. You are supposed henceforth to be limited in religious matters to a certain type of people, a certain set of ideas, and even to a certain social class, whereas until you joined a church you had no such prejudices. Accordingly while people have a great respect for the name Christian they have much less respect for terms such as Catholic, Presbyterian, Anglican, Methodist, which imply a sectional loyalty. To be proud of these labels is held to be a mark of bigotry. They are, therefore, held to be a reproach which no man of reasonable sympathies would willingly incur or teach other people to incur.

Nevertheless, belonging to *any* society may involve a similar reproach. To be a Conservative makes it appear that you put all Socialists beyond the pale. In universities, to be an "arts" man leads people to assume that you have no knowledge of or sympathy with science. In business, to be in the distributive trades means that you are supposed to keep a watchful eye on producers and importers. To be a parson is to have a barrier placed between you and the layman. In schools, if you become a headmistress you give up membership of the assistant mistresses' association and join another one which excludes your old friends. In all these, and in the Church, too, it will be noticed that there are present two assumptions which are not necessarily true, namely that to be united with people in one interest identifies you with all their other interests, and that to have certain interests different from those of other people puts you out of fellowship with them. It implies broadmindedness towards those within the fellowship and narrowmindedness towards those without. Sometimes, no doubt, it actually is the case that men give preference in one sphere of life to those who are their fellow members in another. Church members, for instance, seek to get members of their own church on to town councils or boards of management of schools.

We do not avoid the reproach, however, by avoiding the fellowship. That, in the case of Christianity, would be to shut oneself out from the most characteristic experiences of our religion. We avoid it only by bearing it and showing that it is not true; that is to say, by redeeming it. This vicariousness is itself part of the Christian view of things. By identifying ourselves with any group of people we run the risk of incurring any odium (and also praise) which attaches to them, even if we ourselves have done nothing to deserve it. There is the continual possibility of misunderstanding, and the way out of it for the Christian is not by argument or by the assertion of claims but by witnessing against it by his attitude. Belonging to a church, therefore, may in itself put us in the way of this spiritual excellence, a quality quite different from the "kudos" of belonging to a great and honourable society. If there is to be any glorying let it be glorying in the Lord alone.

The existence of the local denominational church is thus for thoughtful and sensitive people a "means of grace", an insurance against pride and a way of preventing them from taking refuge in a belief in a church wholly invisible in which loyalties are standardized according to the pattern of the person holding the belief. The church is a society of actual persons here and now, of different ages and sexes, of different temperaments and occupations, of different degrees of intelligence and of spiritual experience, localized in a given place at a given time. That is what the plain man sees and so far the plain man is quite right. It is for the members of that church not to claim that it is something more, but to demonstrate it. It is in this society, and not just in the-church-as-idea, that people ought to be able to discover Christ as a living reality.

Education in church membership is thus in a sense a culmination of all the rest of education in the Christian religion. Yet it often begins simply with habit. Children are associated with a church because their parents are, or because their school is, or because they have friends who go, or

o

because it is the nearest, or because it is a way of getting rid of them for an hour or two on Sundays (let us be realists in these matters!).   In other words this association like many others just "happens".   It may continue simply as a social custom, or it may be given a meaning.

In education in religion use should be made of this habit of like-minded people to get together.   The like-mindedness may be purely a matter of social tastes, but there is no real sense of cohesion in that.   It needs to be turned into a common loyalty to a cause, or to a leader, and the whole art of running youth clubs on religious lines is concerned with effecting this transformation.   It is this side of church membership that appeals to the adventurous and the thoughtful as well as to the generous spirit of youth.   And it is the leader that matters more than the cause, for to follow a leader not only involves more discipline than supporting a cause, but it is a truer way of being "represented".   You do not take up a leader as you take up a cause: it is he who takes you up, and you do as he tells you, and do it gladly, because he is your representative and not merely your commander.   There is nothing young folk appreciate more than being ordered about by someone in whom they thoroughly believe.

That is what being a member of a church really means. It may begin by being a social act on a not very high level, but it can be educated into discipleship of Christ.   This is something which people may pursue together, but it has meaning for religion only when each person is also pursuing it alone. Churches have often been organized too much after the manner of the earlier feudal system, in which a man gave allegiance only to the overlord of his own immediate community, and these overlords themselves gave allegiance to others who gave theirs to the king.   There is a parable in the action of William the Conqueror, who had each several landowner, however small, also to give personal allegiance direct to himself.

The discipline of the society is one that young people easily understand and appreciate.   The scoutmaster who himself does well all that the scouts themselves do only fairly well, and who never asks them to do anything that he is not willing to do himself, is a symbol of this type of loyalty. Never to presume upon superior gifts or abilities as if they exempted one from the ordinary tasks of discipleship is a characteristic of the man who is disciplined by his loyalty. Boys and girls honour this kind of thing, and because of it they often choose as their heroes in school not the person whose ability in games is the despair of everyone else, but some other person who carries other gifts with self-forgetfulness.

The young have an uncanny intuition for humility in other people, and they may think of it as a purely temperamental thing. It is therefore part of religious education to show them where it comes from. "Have this mind in you," says the Apostle, "which was also in Christ Jesus; who, being in the form of God, counted it not a thing to be grasped to be on an equality with God, but emptied himself, taking the form of a servant, and being found in fashion as a man he humbled himself, becoming obedient even unto death." The Sacrament of the Lord's Supper is not only a showing forth of the Lord's death until He come but is a symbol of the society brought into being by this kind of love. Hence this society is not only a sign of grace but also a means of grace.

7

The Christian society, like every other society, upholds the people in it and keeps before them a standard below which they might easily fall. The fact that other people are aware of your position and expect you to live up to it may not be the highest motive for doing right, but it is certainly a motive, and in those "dry seasons" of the soul it may be the only motive. Religion, as we have seen, is at bottom a matter of feeling, of intuition, of insight. But what if the feeling is not there and the vision is dim? Are these the tokens that God is no longer present, and that the periods of insight were periods of delusion? Younger people are apt to think so, just as when they fall in love they think that life should be one long sweet song, and they are apt to resent discords and silences. Membership of the society helps to tide us over these shallows, and if we are unable to make vows for ourselves, vows are made for us. It is a help, therefore, to have something public about membership of a society in order that expectations may be aroused which for very shame we would not like to disappoint. Boy Scouts and Girl Guides make their promise in the presence of their fellows, in some schools children are made prefects in the presence of the whole school, and this makes everybody concerned with the vocation of those whose profession is thus publicly acknowledged.

But the Christian society is not confined to *the* or to *a* visible church. The writer to the Hebrews exhorts his readers to lay aside every weight and the sin which so easily besets them "seeing we are compassed about with so great a cloud of witnesses". These witnesses were those in the past who had testified to a faith but had not "received the promise". Nothing is more characteristic of temptation than the sense of loneliness which it brings. It is one of the embarrassments that older boys and girls feel when they consult an older person, because it seems to them that they are so different from other people and that no one has been tempted like this before. And then when they have given way to it they feel keenly that they are cut off from the society of all decent people, even though no one may know about it except themselves. This is no delusion, sin really does cut off people from the fullest kind of sympathy with their fellows, and it is just as true of the older person whose sin may be a presumptuous familiarity with divine things as of the youth who gives way in secret to masturbation.

This segregating effect of temptation has somehow to be overcome, for in sensitive minds it is apt to lead to the idea that there is no hope for them and that they can never be any better. It is here that the sense of a "cloud of witnesses" is helpful. The visible society may help a man to observe standards of outward (and even of inward) conduct which he has publicly acknowledged, but the invisible society is also a support. Among the documents of the faith, along with the Scriptures, there are the stories of Christian witness all down the ages, that "communion of saints" in which the past and the present are united in fellowship. The calling to mind of those who have passed on is not a merely historical exercise, it is a recollection of their concern for the warfare in which we ourselves are still engaged.

The "grace of God" is the name given by Paul to this enabling power, and all the apparently complicated language of the epistles is simply an attempt to set forth what it is and how it works. When we think of the state of education among the common people in the ancient world, in the servants' quarters in a Roman household and in the streets of Ephesus, is it not curious that the people who first received Paul's epistles knew quite well what he was talking about, while far better educated people of our own day think of them as incomprehensible and unnecessary word-spinning? These letters and, if you like, this system of doctrine, spoke to the condition of these simple people as nothing else, not even the Gospels themselves, spoke to it. And, still more remarkable, wherever this Gospel has been preached, in Africa or India, in the Middle Ages or today, Paul's way of expounding it has spoken to the deepest needs of men. These doctrines are not accretions on the simple Gospel; they *are* the simple Gospel. It was Christ who died and rose again who—to use the old phraseology—"brought life and immortality to light".

8

This, of course, brings with it a sense of responsibility, for if a man feels himself to be a member of a great and honourable society, living or dead, he will not wish to let it down, nor will he wish to let himself down in his own eyes. But apart altogether from seasons of temptation there are also times when decisions have to be made. The glow of human fellowship has departed, perhaps because we have come

home to our ordinary duties after the thrill of a summer camp
or conference, and when we are alone we have decisions to
make which might have seemed easy during the emotional
uplift of life together. Here the sense of membership of a
still greater invisible society will help us to decide rightly.
This is not because we feel ourselves to be part of a company
(after all, that may be mere wishful thinking) but because
recognition of this society makes us to be representative
people. We are not mere individuals deciding this way or
that according to our own individual convenience, we are
representatives: what we do the society does, and our sense
of the society helps to determine what we do.

It is a truth so true that it is often caricatured, that an
Englishman who loves his country and is carrying out some
piece of work alone in a foreign land will seek to act not just
as an individual but as the ideal Englishman would act. The
invisible society is a guide and an inspiration to him. And this
is true of any honest person of any nation or of any well-
defined group. Thus we are at one and the same time saved
from that devastating kind of responsibility of appearing to
make decisions in a vacuum, unrelated to anybody and anything, and at the same time are given that sense of responsibility which comes from realizing that we are not here simply
to please ourselves. The chart of life which we need when
camp is broken up and the tumult and the shouting have died
is not a syllabus which we are left to make for ourselves
without any help at all—it is something with which those
who have gone before us are concerned. Mere unrelated
individualism is therefore a state which is rather less than
human, whether we are afraid to fall into it or whether we
seek to cultivate it. "Ye are not your own", says the New
Testament again and again. And the fact that we belong to
God is brought home to us almost more through the communion of saints than in any other way. It is from this side
that education in religion can best stress the idea of the
solemn trust of life.

CHAPTER XI

THE EDUCATION OF THE EMOTIONS:
(2) WORSHIP

I

THE characteristic activity of religion is worship—indeed it is the characteristic of man himself. He is the only worshipping animal. In Christianity, however, this urge to worship is often obscured because the Gospel has proved to be so powerful an incentive to social justice and to give so adequate an explanation of the deepest nature of man that a personal relationship to God Himself has often appeared to be unnecessary.

There are, no doubt, some people for whom work really is prayer and not just a substitute for it, and for all of us in some moods even the substitute is better than nothing, but this attitude misses the true nature not only of religion but also of Christian service. Religion is concerned with the unseen world and at all levels we are aware of it in times of deep emotion. It may be in the thrill of dark, nameless fear, or it may be in

> that serene and blessed mood
> In which the affections gently lead us on . . .
> While with an eye made quiet by the power
> Of harmony, and the deep power of joy
> We see into the life of things.

As we have already noticed, the purpose of education in religion is to inform this feeling, but it often happens that the form itself becomes more important than the feeling which it informs. We are more concerned with doctrine or Biblical history on the one hand, or with practical conduct on the other, than we are with the primary drive towards the unseen which gives vigour and direction to both. The nature of God, rather than God Himself, becomes the object of our seeking, or we try to do the "right thing" without reference to God who alone makes the thing to be right.

We thus meet again the dilemma in religious education. Knowledge and conduct are both of them obvious matters for instruction, and, given an understanding of the subject and of the pupil, it is not difficult to learn how to teach them. But neither of them has necessarily anything to do with religion, although they may and do use its language. Education in these matters alone is not education in religion. Yet how can feelings be "educated" and still remain feelings? Once you have explained a thrill it ceases to be a thrill. This result may be highly satisfactory to the people who separate off thinking from feeling, and assume the former to be a "higher" activity of mankind, but it deprives life of colour and also of significance. We thus relate life to nothing except the product of our own thinking and doing. We favour the closed circle within which all is known, foreseen and inevitable, and yet which, in reference to the sum of things, may have no significance whatever.

Nevertheless, we come back to the practical point whether religion in the personal, emotional sense is at all necessary. Is it not, as the Positivists believe, a stage which is left behind by man in his climb out of savagery? And are not the assured ethical results of it sufficient? Do not the view of social life given to us by Amos and the unknown prophet of the Exile and the principles laid down in the Sermon on the Mount provide a thoroughly sound basis for any permanent human society? J. M. Keynes' *Economic Consequences of the Peace* (1919) is an admirable commentary in economic terms on the law of forgiveness as laid down in Christianity, and as every one of his prophecies has come true why need we go back to any transcendental origin of this sentiment? May we not apply the discoveries of religion without ourselves taking the trouble to discover them all over again?

And in the same way with regard to conduct. "Of what

doth it avail" (to repeat again Thomas à Kempis) "if I argue learnedly concerning the Trinity but lack compassion, and so am displeasing to the Trinity?" We should agree, but is the converse also true? As long as we have compassion and are apparently pleasing to the Trinity, need we bother about the Trinity at all?

This familiar method of argument sets up alternatives where no alternatives really exist. It is quite true that thinking and doing can both be carried on satisfactorily without reference to the unseen world, just as it is possible to run a wireless shop and mend a customer's set without knowing anything about physics. But somewhere, and held by somebody, there must be a grasp of first principles. The application of the thing is not the thing itself, and if unusual circumstances arise, our knowledge of applications alone will not help us. And in the case of religion "first principles" means contact with the unseen world. There is mystery on both sides of knowledge, at the beginning and at the end, but they are a different kind of mystery. The first is due to the absence of knowledge, and the second to its perfection. At the beginning that which we do not understand is a "mystery" to us, and it is cleared up by thought and knowledge, but at the end the "mystery" is that it should be at all. To the merely plodding thinker mystery is a nuisance which it is the purpose of learning to abolish: but to the great scientist or philosopher and to the religious man, mystery is the home of his spirit. In other words education leads us to the point at which its method of approach is no longer applicable, and the later we are in arriving at that point the more convinced we are of its truth.

We might take an illustration from that familiar condition known as "falling in love". The relations between the young people may have begun with a common interest in hobbies or work or social standards or a hundred and one external associations through which they have got to know one another. But "falling in love" is not in the least a continuation of this process, it is a different *kind* of thing altogether and cannot be explained in terms of "interests" at all. It may be present even where interests are diverse. It is an attitude of the person himself.

So it is with all sound knowledge—it issues in mystery and almost in a negation of itself, and yet the knowledge is the more perfect just because of this. It grasps reality no longer in bits and pieces but as a whole. And at this stage it becomes religious. At a lower level there is no doubt a sharp contrast between knowledge and feeling, but the way of life is found not by clinging to the one and despising the other but by pursuing either to the point where the other is present as well.

It is the same in regard to conduct. At ordinary levels conduct can be and often is a code which we observe, and as such it has nothing necessarily to do with religion. But religion is concerned with higher (and deeper) levels, and here conduct is no longer the following of rules, it is something which expresses our attitude to the universe. At this higher level dualisms are discovered which are not even dreamed of earlier. We remember that Bunyan's insight placed a by-way to hell under the very slopes of the Delectable Mountains as well as by the entrance to the Celestial City. It is only when conduct is a progressive attitude that we find ourselves at some time or other in a region where the choice is not so much between this or that action as between taking sides with God or the devil. And sin is not against our fellow men only—it is against God, it is the King's peace that we are breaking, and it is only in God that we can do the right thing. It is no self-deception that makes the saint much more sensitive to his own sin than the sinner is to his; it is due to a greater awareness of the purpose of God in whose sight all our righteousness is as filthy rags.

Education in religion, therefore, if it is to lead to worship, must not only cultivate "natural religion" but must also carry Christian instruction and Christian ethics into those regions in which God not only is a necessity for thought but is Himself a reality, and is found to be taking the initiative. At a certain stage of experience God is able to do things with us and for us that He is not able to do earlier. It may be that this is one of the compensations, for instance, of deep sorrow. It brings us, if we will, into a world of spirit altogether different from the world which we normally inhabit. We find a purpose running through the past, everything that we have done or known seems to have led up to this point, and in this Valley of Humiliation after wrestling with Apollyon we have found ourselves in the presence of God.

2

We need, therefore, to notice the connection between religious worship and religious belief. A good deal of worship is a thrill; the dim religious light, the traditional ritual, the exultation of music, the suggestiveness of architecture, the fascination of corporate silence, or the spaciousness of a landscape under the open sky—all these seem to work upon the emotions and produce a sense of unseen reality. While this is certainly religious it is not necessarily Christian, for it may be divorced from both Christian thought and Christian practice.

But there is also another side to worship. It is a positive affirmation of the presence of the divine. Conduct is affected by habits or moods, knowledge may change with further thought, but here is something which is not so much dependent on personal considerations. Its very externalism (even in a Quaker meeting) is important, and it is altogether a mistake to confine the value of worship to the consciousness of the person taking part in it. There must be sincerity, but it need not always be consciously present in any particular worshipper, or even in any particular celebrant. It may be altogether an act of faith, a belief that this represents what we know to be true, even though at the moment we cannot prove it, nor even feel ourselves to be in the mood for it. To make religious observance dependent on mood or on fashion would surely be a form of materialism, and would reduce God to the status of a subjective disturbance. It has always been a weakness of Protestantism that it over-emphasizes the importance of being conscious of what is taking place.

Sometimes it is worship itself that makes us conscious.

This question of "consciousness" makes, however, a difference between the worship of adults and that of children. The adult, even when he is not in the mood for it, can nevertheless come as an act of faith, knowing that moods are not everything, and resting on the affirmation which worship suggests. The child is not in that position, and the attempt to induce "reverence" by telling him of the unseen presence of God and all that it means shows a misunderstanding of a child's nature. If the surroundings are properly suggestive the child will need little telling, for his spiritual life is much less choked by the cares of this world and the deceitfulness of riches than the life of the adult. As the aim is to educate the emotions the method is by suggestion rather than instruction, for worship depends on atmosphere rather than on articulation. Yet, as in other kinds of æsthetic appreciation, all people are not suggestible to the same extent or to the same things. The crudity of the Salvation Army "citadels" may strike a jarring note for more cultivated tastes, yet it may more truly bring God home to the hearts and consciences of some worshippers than a service ordered with more subtlety. People are not necessarily lacking in spiritual sensitiveness because they prefer Tennyson to Gerard Manley Hopkins. Nevertheless, there can be education in worship.

The word "atmosphere", as we have seen in an earlier chapter, has often the unfortunate effect of making people assume that worship is something that comes of itself. The wind bloweth where it listeth, and to try to arrange for its blowing is to fall into the error of formalism. This I believe to be a profound misunderstanding of what worship really is. It is not a kind of formless thrill with which we are left after we have put our intellects to sleep. It is rather the gathering together of all that we have learned and known about God and Christ through the Bible, the Church, the long roll of human history and the natural universe, together with all that we appreciate of beauty in art and music deepened and purified through human love and social responsibility, into a corporate act of praise and prayer to God who is the source of all these things. It is analogous in its effect to music. Music is the most direct and moving of all the arts, and yet its technique is the most intellectual. It is built up out of a complicated system of mathematical relationship of notes and tones and instruments. Yet all this fuses into an emotion which is the deeper and more compelling because of its intellectual quality.

Corporate worship is of the same nature. It needs careful preparation and arrangement, although the greatest art here, as everywhere else, is to conceal art. It is a matter not so much of adornment as of things done decently and in order, and this is most necessary with children. They dislike uncertainty, a sense of not being sure of what is going to happen. Those who arrange worship, therefore, not only should have a plan themselves but should ensure that the worshipper understands it. The misery which some Nonconformists suffer when they attend the parish church and cannot find their way about the prayer-book, or the acute discomfort of some Anglicans in a united service when some layman gets up to pray and may say anything, are instances of the insecurity that gets in the way of worship. Children feel it intensely. They are ritualistic in play as well as in other activities, and like things done not only in order but in the same order. That which appears to the adult to be mere formalism is often to the child full of suggestiveness.

The adolescent is a special case. He is beginning to enquire and criticize, and everything, including worship, has to give a reason for itself. At the same time he has become susceptible to beauty, and has often developed a sense of unworthiness in its presence which causes him profound distress. Both of these attitudes may be present together or one of them may prevail over the other. He may seek to worship God either alone in church or in external nature where he can decide on his own ritual, or else in the ornate surroundings of some "high church" service. He may privately burn incense in his room and secretly read *The Garden of the Soul*. On the other hand, if he has been brought up in this kind of way already he may react against it in favour of the austerity of a Quaker meeting.

3

School worship, therefore, like church services for children, is difficult to organize where there is a wide age range. Yet it needs organizing with the utmost care. Quiet and orderliness are essential. If the visible surroundings are suggestive more of the day's work than of anything else, there should be in view something which is symbolic of a different context, even if it be only a vase of flowers. Hymns need to be carefully chosen, and it is quite a mistake to seek out only those that are called "children's hymns". "Little drops of water, little grains of sand" is not more suitable to a child's tender years than "O God our help in ages past" sung to the tune "St. Anne". Somehow it usually happens that in this regard day schools are less likely to play down to the children than Sunday schools. Tunes need to be chosen within the children's compass, and on the whole it is as important to choose the right tunes as to choose the right words. This is the occasion for great passages from the Bible and elsewhere to be read carefully and with disciplined expression, for the sound of the language makes an earlier appeal than the sense of it. Nothing is more worshipful than beautiful reading. It will be found that children learn passages by heart without effort if they are attracted by the sound and if they hear them often enough, and, if I might use a familiar and psychologically inaccurate metaphor, one of the happiest possessions that anyone can have is a mind "stored" with the sonorous English of the Authorized Version.

It is well to see that no passages are learned with a view to reproduction before admiring elders.

The relation between school assembly and the Scripture lesson is important. If the children hear in worship a passage which they meet in the context of study, each activity will help to inform the other. Where Bible-reading is isolated from study of the Bible, would-be broadminded people often become obsessed with the habit of supplementing the Bible with other literature, particularly from other religions. But literature used in this way is a matter of context much more than of texts, and while a quotation from the *Bhagavad-Gita* may look extraordinarily like a passage from St. John's Gospel, their respective contexts show them to be utterly different. In the modern Scripture lesson the Bible is studied in its context of history and experience, and this ought to make more effective its liturgical use in school assembly. But if literature from other religions is used for liturgical purposes it ought elsewhere to be subjected to the same critical treatment as the Bible. A great deal depends on why it is used. As an illustration it may be excellent, but as an exhibition of the broadmindedness of the conductor of worship it may introduce a self-conscious element which spoils the worship.

In the same way in the Scripture lesson to substitute for an intensive study of, say, a Hebrew prophetic book or a Pauline epistle in its context of history and literature a superficial study of what is called "comparative religion" is educationally a poor exchange. It replaces appreciation by information. And there is a bigotry of broadmindedness as well as a bigotry of narrowmindedness. To some people it is a matter of self-congratulation to insist that in the sacred books of other religions there are things that are "as good as" anything in the parables or in the book of Psalms. This competitive use of religious texts is of all attitudes the least religious. We can maintain this judgement even while recognizing the low spiritual value of much that is in the Bible and the high spiritual value of much that is outside it.

The importance of contexts comes out again where people feel that the creeds ought to be brought up to date and expressed in present-day language. There is an obvious case for this, although in a sense it is always being done, even in the Church of Rome. The faith is continually being expounded in modern terms.[1] But a creed is a short statement used, no doubt, in a catechism but chiefly used in a liturgy, and needing for its interpretation the context of history. To take

[1] See R. A. Knox. *The Mass in Slow Motion.*

it out of that context and to re-write it in every generation would be as unhistorical as to treat as verbally inspired the present form independent of a context altogether. Moreover, for liturgical uses a historic form of words is of the greatest value. It is around this that the accreted memories of the ages have gathered, and in worship the sense of history is psychologically as suggestive as the sense of beauty.

Ought school worship to be compulsory? From what I have already said about the connection between worship and moods it is clear that the answer will be "yes". As we have already seen, the most notable characteristic of education is that the appreciation of it is a product of it, and on this fact rests the whole case for compulsion up to a certain age. Corporate worship is, I believe, in exactly the same position. If people wish to worship no question arises, but we may ask, Why should they be made to worship if they do not want to do it? The reply is that they are not being made to worship, any more than compulsory education means that the child is being made to learn. They are being made to be present, and are thereby being put in the way of worship. What then follows lays a great responsibility upon the people who have the power to compel, for their aim, like that of the teacher, should be to make compulsion unnecessary. Compulsion in worship ought to be viewed as a necessary stage, equally unpleasant while it lasts to the teacher as to the pupil.

4

The relation of worship to discipline and conduct is very close. It is as conduct issues from worship that it is kept free from egotism. Doing the right thing oneself, or doing good to others, is to run the risk of Pharisaism, and may easily lead to the idea that the Almighty ought to be obliged to us for being so virtuous. This is not always recognized either in school mottoes or in Speech Day addresses. Altruism may easily become a substitute for religious loyalty or else a purely theological virtue performed in meritorious obedience to some ordinance about alms-giving. Both of these attitudes are rooted in self-interest, and result in self-flattery. It is only as we see things in the presence of God that we get the perspective right, and it is only as action is a function of spiritual life and springs out of it that it is purged of self-centredness.

For the adolescent at a critical age, and for all of us in the throes of those "adolescent" periods which keep cropping up throughout one's life, worship is an affirmation not only of truth but also of goodness. In translating thought into action there is often a kind of dead-centre from which it is just as easy to fall into righteousness as into sin. Economic and social advantages may be enough to pull the balance down on the wrong side, while the environment of worship makes it easier to do the right. Worship is thus of value to conduct as well as to belief, for it assists the mood in which we can, if we will, look out on life with the eyes of God. And this is as true of problems of thought as of personal temptations.

> When I thought how I might know this
> It was too painful for me;
> Until I went into the sanctuary of God.

5

Corporate worship, however, is only one side of worship. It is concerned equally with the person as with the community. Prayer is to the individual what corporate worship is to the group, and education in prayer is part of education in religion. How can it be done?

It is here where a philosophy of prayer is necessary. What are we doing when we pray? What ought we to pray for? Is prayer necessary at all? For very many Christian people today prayer has altogether gone out of fashion.

Teaching to pray depends on one's idea of God. If He is thought of as omnipotent and omnipresent, a being whose nod sways the universe, prayer will mean asking for things in the attitude of a suppliant at His feet and from time to time begging

P

for mercy. "Less than the dust beneath thy chariot wheel."
A good many hymns encourage this attitude, and it certainly
brings a pleasant thrill of self-abnegation. Yet somehow this
does not appear to be the view of Jesus or of the great prophets.
God's relation to men is not that of a Führer to his subjects.
It is that of a mother to a family of interesting, independent
and often wayward children. They have sprung from her life,
and are what they are because of her sacrifice. She exhibits
love at all times, but love may show itself in sternness and
discipline. On their part they can always take her love for
granted although they may not always know, or, when they do
know, approve of how it is going to work. Yet when they do
realize the depth and wisdom of it and the sacrifice it means to
her, it constrains them towards her by a force that nothing
can break. Sin becomes more sinful in the eyes of the child
just because the mother—marvellous to relate—refuses on her
part to allow it to destroy this love. The prodigal son in the
parable asks not for forgiveness but for punishment, and so he
finds forgiveness.

If God is like this, as Jesus declared and showed Him to be,
prayer cannot be a matter of asking for things, so to speak,
"out of the blue". It is certainly concerned with petition, but
much more with the establishment on our part of the child's
relationship within the family. It is the mother and father that
are appreciated rather than the gifts they bring. But children
do not find this out all at once, and even in the best regulated
families they go through a stage of esteeming the gifts far
more than the giver. And the human family is exactly the
same towards God.

Education in prayer begins with the habit in early childhood of "saying prayers". No doubt all sorts of questions
will be asked of the parents, but children are often much more
understanding of the right relationship to God than are their
well-meaning elders who work so hard at "clearing up their
difficulties". And in matters of the spirit the understanding
of an activity is obtained along with the practice of the
activity itself—otherwise there are no data to go upon.

Despise not habits. They are a convenient framework within which to build up something better, but they are still there when we become tired of building.

Forms too are useful. Even the sturdiest opponent of liturgical prayer will exempt the Lord's Prayer and will have it taught to his children. But at a later stage children and adults too are in regard to prayer in the position of small children writing a letter. They "never know what to say". To begin, therefore, with words supplied by somebody else, but which speak to their condition, does not substitute form for reality but is a way of ensuring reality. The Psalms have been used in this manner all through the Christian centuries, and many of the "offices" of the Church are but commentaries on certain psalms. The Book of Common Prayer is part of the spiritual heritage of all English-speaking Christians, and the stately language of the collects not only provides words for our own aspirations but also the atmosphere in which those aspirations can become more expressive.

O Almighty God, who alone canst order the unruly wills and affections of sinful men; Grant unto thy people, that they may love the things which thou commandest, and desire that which thou dost promise: that so, among the sundry and manifold changes of the world, our hearts may surely there be fixed, where true joys are to be found; through Jesus Christ our Lord.

In dry seasons, when faith is dim and life is hard, to be able to fall back on such language as this even as a habit is to ensure not only that the mood will return but also that whether it is present or not we can nevertheless carry on. Some denominations use their hymn books in this way, while collections such as A Chain of Prayer Across the Ages are familiar to most people.

In these ways we help ourselves to recollect God into whose presence we wish to come, and so talk with Him as we would with one who we know loves us "beyond all that we can ask or think", and whom we seek to love. All longing, all petition, all self-examination, all meditation and every other aspect of the deepest need of our hearts are thus seen in the light of God.

P*

CHAPTER XII

FUNDAMENTAL AIMS

I

Having looked at the various factors involved in religious education we are now in a position to attempt a statement of its fundamental aims.

It is clear that the specific aims of religious education vary according to the type of school or church or even individual concerned. It may be concerned with the making of church members, or the propagation of a cause, or the stimulation of a higher standard of morality or the presentation of a cultural background to life. High-brows, low-brows, propagandists of every description, sectarians, doctrinaires, Church-and-State men, and latitudinarians have all at some point an interest in this subject and have sought to mould it to their hearts' desire. If, however, it is to be separated from proselytism and evangelism on the one hand and the edification of the faithful on the other, its fundamental aims must be strictly educational, that is to say it must grade its subject matter according to its own development and the mental development of the people intended to receive it, it must afford an examination of contexts and a correlation with other sides of life, it must call for criticism and independent conviction as to its conclusions, which it must be able to present as a whole picture.

Clearly, therefore, religious education in school has two aspects. It is an education in itself and there are, as we have seen, sound educational reasons why it should be a subject in every school. But it is also preparatory to the fullness of the Christian experience, both personal and corporate. The challenge that is inherent in it is one which the teacher should neither give nor avoid. It is inherent in the subject matter properly taught, and to attempt to emphasize it apart from that subject matter is to go beyond purely educational requirements. In the Council schools of England there are two good reasons why this should be avoided. In the first place, the children in the Council schools are compelled to be present, and they represent all kinds of homes, religious of various sorts and non-religious, and the schools of the nation ought not to be used for propaganda purposes. Secondly, the fullness of the Christian faith requires some *permanent* community in which to exercise itself and develop, and the school cannot produce that community. It is not itself a church, nor is it linked with a church. And even in schools that are denominational, whether Catholic or Protestant, the educational aim and the aim of church membership are differing aims, and the second should not be allowed to get in the way of the first before the proper time arrives.

The time when this should happen will be determined by the pupil's own development and the natural development of the subject. Over-anxiety, obsession with "orthodoxy" (a term quite out of place in educational circles), morbid concern for the pupil's spiritual welfare, may result before its time in the acceptance of a position determined by authority, but it will not be well grounded and it cannot be called educational.

2

In searching, therefore, for our fundamental aims we must recall that the centre of Christian education is Christ. It is not the Assyrian empire, nor the Graeco-Roman world, nor the canon of Scripture, nor the Church, nor St. Paul. This does not mean, for example, that the Old Testament should be searched for proof texts of a later revelation or that the epistles are an "accretion" on the pure gospel. These are inorganic ways of viewing what is really a living question. It means rather that Christ's life and death and continued influence are the *religious* standards by which everything in this religion is to be judged. The reason why there is any Church history at all or any New Testament, or why the Old Testament means so much to us, is because of Christ. He is the norm of human psychology as well as the revelation of God to man, and so all that human beings, prophet, priest, pope or layman, ever think, plan or do has to stand at the bar of His judgement. Whether Paul was or was not referring to the future life when he said, "We must all stand at the judgement seat of Christ", it is nevertheless true of the present world of persons as we know it, whether in history or in experience.

Now the nature of Christ Himself is a doctrinal question and there is a variety of views. It has been discussed hitherto not sufficiently in psychological and far too much in meta-physical terms, but in any case this does not come strictly within the educational field. Nor does the question of the personal acceptance of Christ as Lord and Leader. These two matters, although fundamental to the Christian religion, are not fundamental to Christian education as such. They cannot be kept out altogether, but it is not the teacher's business to emphasize them. If they arise naturally, as they will, and the teacher is asked about them, he should give his answer as a private person and not as an official of the school. In a denominational school he may, however, be required to reverse the process and to give the official answer without intruding his personal views. This latter situation, it will be seen, has no relation to the educational process, whereas the former has.

3

Given the centrality of Christ in religious education there are two corollaries from it which will provide us with two fundamental aims. The first is that He is the revelation not only of God to men but also of man to man. The second is that He treated the world as His Father's house.

I have already spoken of Christ as the norm of human life. It is for lack of such a norm that so much of the study of psychology goes astray. Books are written on "abnormal" psychology without any indication of the norm from which this is a deviation. We are indeed often left with the conclusion that psychology is largely a subjective study based on the assurance that the writer of the psychology book himself is normal, but no one else. A study of the earlier personal history of a good many psychologists would indicate that psychological systems are a rationalization of the author's own way of life. This reference to contexts is a healthy corrective to that sense of intimidation which a too credulous acceptance of their systems is apt to produce. We cannot give up the verbal inspiration of *Genesis* merely to accept the verbal inspiration of Freud.

It will, therefore, be a fundamental aim of religious education to bring out this discovery of the true nature of man through the work of Christ. And there are not one but several ways of doing this and they are all needed. A study of the Gospels themselves is, of course, primary, but we have to remember here as elsewhere that they were written because Christ meant so much more to people than the story of a great teacher. We have therefore carefully to notice the effect He had on the people who believed in Him and who had never seen Him. The Christ of the Epistle to the Colossians is as necessary for the complete picture as the Jesus of Mark's Gospel.

It should be noted also how this testimony has been repeated all down the ages. It has cut across the limited witness of every nation, age and denomination. The English Baptist servant girl, Agnes Beaumont,[1] writes of it in 1674 in language much the same as that of St. Bernard in the twelfth century and the Japanese Kagawa in the twentieth.

Then we must further take into account the effect He has had on the people who did *not* believe in Him. The idea of the irresistible effect of His personality leaves out of account the fact that Judas resisted it, as did Caiaphas, and that the

[1] *The Narrative of the Persecution of Agnes Beaumont in 1674*, edited from the MS. in the British Museum, by G. B. Harrison.

Jerusalem mob hounded Him to His death. There is no warrant in Scripture for the belief that if only you treat bad people with love they will at once turn from their evil ways. On the other hand there is every corroboration in psychology for the "Johannine" view that the very presence of Christ in the world was a judgement upon the world. Littlefaith gained more faith, but Mr. Badman became more evil. It is of the nature of evil not so much to be attracted by goodness as to resent it and to seek to put it out of the way and out of sight. Bill Sikes striking down Nancy is a modern parable of one of the unexpected relationships of good and evil.

When, therefore, the old Evangelicals declared that "it was my sin that nailed him to the tree" they were saying something about Christ which is completely in accord with what we know of the real heart of man. This is not a historical event only. It is a revelation of man throughout all history. It is as alarming as it is unexpected and the "natural" man still finds it difficult to accept. The events of the last twenty years, however, should have made it easier to believe. The fantastic tricks that men have played before high Heaven should convince anyone of the evil that is latent in the human heart. The willingness of men to hand themselves over to leaders who evoke the worst and not the best in them is in itself a wrongdoing, so that people have got to be emancipated from this blind emotional acceptance of leadership as part of their deliverance from sin. Is not this a judgement on all who accept totalitarian leadership, whether in churches or in nations? They are victims of a comforting but illusory belief in the transfer of responsibility.

This, however, is not the only way in which Jesus shows us man as he is. There is a further and apparently contradictory way.

It has always been felt as a difficulty in Freud's psychology, to some extent avoided by Jung, that he is dealing all the while with averages and not with the type. He has no place for that creative activity of men which differentiates individuals from one another, and he is seeking all the time for a kind of lowest common measure of humanity. This confusion of the average with the typical is a very common fallacy. Grant for the sake of argument Freud's contention that the deep-seated drives which all men have in common both among themselves and with animals are the food-getting instinct and the sex instinct, what nearer are we to understanding human nature? It is not until we discover the type that we can understand organisms or persons or institutions, and the type is as likely to be discovered in one as in a million. It needs no more than one Shakespeare to give England her place in the world's literature, and it needs no more than one Christ to demonstrate our real intrinsic humanity.

If we agree with Aristotle that the true nature of an organism is to be found in its highest development, clearly one of the defects of the doctrine of evolution as popularly understood is that it is concerned more with origins than with culminations. Even if we take the purely Pelagian view of Christ's person (and how the orthodox have always delighted in misunderstanding it!) Christ is unique in that He alone is the type to which all others only approximate. And it is a matter of ordinary psychology that the reason why we only approximate is because of the sin which so constantly besets both us and the society of which we are part. There is no need to make this a dogma divorced from any context. It is plain to be seen in every human life and in the life of the whole.

Christ's uniqueness, therefore, is a demonstrably moral uniqueness. It is a matter of character. What metaphysical uniqueness there may be is, and can only be, a matter of speculation, but it is worth noting that a metaphysical uniqueness such as would arise from a miraculous physical birth is not only undemonstrable but if it were demonstrated would neutralize His moral uniqueness. The character of Christ, therefore, is not only the test we apply to the reliability of the Gospel narrative (see page 77) but also the test we apply to the speculations of theologians and philosophers. And if it be said that the character of Christ is no more demonstrable by history than it is by metaphysics, the answer is that we look for it not in the first century only but in those people all down the ages until now whose lives have been remade into a closer conformity to this divine pattern. It is this which is the "raw material" of the theologian.

And in all this we have not departed from the legitimate field of religious education, for it all arises out of a deeper understanding of the Old and New Testaments. Not one student in a hundred will ever appreciate it, but to afford the opportunity of appreciating it is nevertheless a fundamental aim of religious education.

The reference to the *Old* Testament in this context may seem somewhat irrelevant, but educationally it is quite fundamental. And the reason, as we have seen, is not because of "proof texts" pointing to Christ, nor because of some esoteric or allegorical meaning which some modern scholars wish to put upon it. The Old Testament history and religion are the background of the message of Jesus, and, more than that, the Gospel may be said to be, in part at any rate, a recovery of the Old Testament. The prophet over against the priest, the lay element in religion over against the professional, inwardness over against outwardness, the moral over against the ceremonial, the spiritual over against the material, were ideas that were central to the message of Christ as they were central in the great days of Hebrew prophecy to which He constantly referred. And just because the social implications of these great ideas were seen by the prophets not in abstraction but in the day-to-day life of an actual society, those who were the creators of our New Testament did not feel it necessary to go over all that ground again. They took it for granted. They concentrated on the great new fact which was not so much additional to Old Testament prophecy as the power which made it capable of fulfilment. And this fulfilment had a personal as well as a social reference, although both are brought together in the New Testament conception of the Kingdom of God. The Psalms are books of that Old Testament personal religion which again found its culmination but not its supersession in Christ. The Psalmists diagnosed the spiritual maladies of man. The full cure came with Jesus Christ. All this forms an organic and historical view of "fulfilment" rather than a mechanical and subjective one. And so the Old Testament is part of the Gospel.

4

The question of the relation of Christ to God is, as we have seen, a matter beyond the limits of religious education as such, but it cannot altogether be avoided. Not only does the Fourth Gospel deal with it throughout but there are certain manuscripts of Mark which begin "The Gospel of Jesus Christ, the Son of God", and there is a famous "Johannine" verse in Matthew xi. 27. These, however, can again be studied in their contexts as indicating Jesus' own attitude and also what the earliest disciples believed Him to be. Neither of these considerations need be made a matter of dogma, for they are contained in the text itself. But what we ourselves think about it and what it means personally to us carry us to a stage beyond the school.

There is, however, an aspect of Jesus' attitude to life which can well be a subject matter of religious education and an indication of one of its fundamental aims. This is His attitude to the universe around us.

It is a commonplace of Christian apologetic that the modern scientific hypothesis of the rationality of the universe finds its counterpart in the first chapter of *Genesis*. There is a principle of uniformity in nature without which everything would be chaos. This, however, to the ancient writer is no blind principle but a living person. "In the beginning" it was God who created the universe and all that therein is. This idea of a creator is the keynote of the Old Testament handling of nature. The concluding chapters of Job are a magnificent panorama of God's work in nature, animate and inanimate. The Psalms are full of it—

—the heavens, thy handiwork,
the moon and the stars which thou hast ordained.

Proverbs is lost in amazement at the wonders of animal instinct. Isaiah feels that something has gone wrong in nature as well as in man and that in the ideal Kingdom of God even the animals will live together in harmony. Deuteronomy (Chapter xxv.) is emphatic that you must not muzzle the ox that treads out the corn. It will be characteristic of the good man, says the book of Job, that he

> will be in league with the stones of the field
> and the beasts of the field shall be at peace with thee.

These ideas are all taken over into the New Testament and appear in the Gospels, although it is characteristic of the robust individuality of the New Testament writers that Paul, for instance, is not himself much moved by it. ("Doth God take care for oxen?" I Corinthians ix. 9.) To Jesus, however, the whole world is His Father's house and there is nothing that is beyond His care. Not a sparrow falls to the ground un-noticed, the lilies of the field are clothed by God although they last but a day, the birds of the air sow not, but our heavenly Father feeds them.[1] The sky is the throne of God, the earth is the footstool of His feet.

Paul views the universe not as a house of God but as a vast system, the purpose of which is to be found in Christ. It is in Him that all things were created, things visible and things invisible, for He is "the first-born of all creation". "All things have been created through him and unto him . . . and in him all things hold together". (Colossians i. 16-17.) This cosmological note is never absent from Paul's thought. To him the meaning of Christ was not exhausted by His dealings with men. The whole earth is involved, not only now but in the far distant past, before ever there was an earth at all.

This no doubt is poetical language, but there is sound psychology behind it as well as a wealth of Christian

---

[1] "I knew that Christ had given me birth
To brother all the souls on earth.
And every bird and every beast
Should share the crumbs broke at the feast."
JOHN MASEFIELD, *The Everlasting Mercy.*

experience. It is characteristic of the human spirit to seek
to give its greatest experiences an ancestry. Predestination
appears to look forwards into the unknown. In reality it
looks backwards and is an interpretation of the known.
When a man falls in love and is caught up into a timeless
sense of happiness it would seem that the whole of his past
history had been leading up to this moment. It is the latest
event in a series but it is the one event which makes of it a
series at all. Before that, life was just a succession of uncon-
nected, meaningless happenings, but now everything can be
seen to be pointing to this one. And so the last in time is the
first in significance and with this you go back to the beginning
of things and everything falls into its proper place. This is
precisely how Paul felt about Christ. He had come to Paul
half-way through his life, but everything now was seen to have
been leading in this direction. But there was more to it than
even the lifetime of Paul himself. The whole universe was
involved. What Paul has seen Christ to be He must have been
since time itself began. Everything acquires new meaning,
and indeed its *true* meaning, in Christ. Nothing has ever
happened or is likely to happen that can be alien to Him.

This is one aspect of what is called doctrinally "the
eternal sonship of Christ". But there is a further consideration
that arises from Christ's place in the universe.

It is well to remember in this scientific age that the
universe tells us nothing whatever about itself. The distances
of the fixed stars, the ages of the geological epochs, the names
and classification of the elements, the formulation of natural
"laws", are every one of them a deposit of men's thinking.
Science is not something present in the external world.
Science is present only in the minds of scientists. And
scientists are men like ourselves. They have to eat and sleep
and work, they have their joys and their sorrows, they suffer
frustration and enjoy achievement, they are liable to disease,
they have their failings and their sins, and like other men they
have parents and become parents in their turn. The scientist's
objectivity in his own specialism does not emancipate him

from these subjective concerns. And it is to man as man that Christ appeals, and the fact that the man is a scientist or a musician or a bricklayer makes no difference whatever—the appeal is the same to all.

The assumption that "science" is a thing in itself over against another thing in itself called "art" and that both are over against another thing in itself called "religion" is a thoroughly unscientific attitude. It is the same human animal dealing with all of them. When the facts of experience are viewed in their internal and external relationships this method of treatment is called "science". When they are viewed as a whole and are appreciated rather than analysed this method of treatment is called "art". When they are viewed in connection with the whole scheme of things, of life and destiny, we have "religion". This, no doubt, is a wild simplification of what is a much more involved situation, but the fact remains that the ultimate common factor in all ages, nations and disciplines is the mind of man. And just because Christ was the norm of humanity He is the factor that links together all thought and all existence. So that Paul's language in the epistle to the Colossians is not so flamboyant as it appears at first sight. There is in it much sober sense. And to present Christ as Paul saw Him, the unifying factor in all this varied world of time and sense, is surely a fundamental aim in religious education at the present day. And it can be done without appealing to dogma at all.

5

There is, as we saw at the beginning, a divergence between the aim of religion and the aim of education, so much so that not only the method but even the very idea of religious education presents us with a dilemma. That the dilemma can be solved it has been the purpose of this book to show. "Exeunt omnia in mysterium", and all educational progress must sooner or later land us at the threshold of the unseen. Indeed it has not properly done its work until that point is reached. But conversely we can work backwards from the threshold of the mystery into the educational process. Every truly religious experience has the effect of stimulating the intelligence as well as the emotions. It unifies a man's life in the same extraordinary way as we have seen Paul's life was unified.

> The station brook to my new eyes
> Was babbling out of Paradise,
> The waters rushing from the rain
> Were singing Christ has risen again.
> I thought all earthly creatures knelt
> From rapture of the joy I felt.[1]

This unification is a vital ingredient of the educated man's mind, but here the educational process is, as it were, short-circuited. To see life steadily and see it whole is the privilege of the Christian even more than it is the achievement of the educated man. As you walk by the sea shore the waters of the ocean are to be found not only beyond the sands but also below your feet if you dig down far enough. This is a not inapt parable of the relations of education and religion. It is the same ocean to be explored and it is the same person who does the exploring, but there are two different ways of doing it.

The man whose life is unified by the Gospel is curious to know what has happened to him. He needs Christian education as well as Christian conversion. His life needs to be informed as well as inspired and unified. The Pauline epistles are to be followed by the Synoptic Gospels. Who is this Christ, this Unknown by whose power men are turned from darkness unto light and from the power of Satan unto God? The Gospels will tell us the story. But we shall need also to know why the story began where it did and when it did, and the psalms and the prophets will amplify the story itself.

Consequently religious education has a twofold reference. Its concern is to inform the minds of those who have already

---

[1] John Masefield. *The Everlasting Mercy.*

come to Christ but know very little about the Christian faith, and it has also to be the schoolmaster (*paidagogos*) to lead other people, particularly children, to Christ. It is a corroboration of the Gospel and also a preparation for the Gospel. In neither case is the educational method a substitute for the Gospel, but it is its fundamental aim to lead people to the point where the Gospel takes hold upon, or, to use Pauline language, "apprehends", them. And the Gospel itself will provide a further education of the mind.

God is his own interpreter
And he will make it plain.

INDEX

The Garden City Press Limited, Letchworth, Herts